MW00817262

Voice and Valor

An Autobiography for Re-humanization

Dante A. Payton

Published in Richmond, VA, for Spirit 'n Life
Books.

The Bible versions used in this publication were
accessed, respectively, through
https://www.biblegateway.com.

Author's first name is used while pseudonyms for
autobiographical vignettes for protection of privacy.

Printed in the United States of America.
ISBN-13: 978-0692144886
ISBN-10: 0692144889

Voice and Valor

CONTENTS

Voice and Valor

Acknowledgements

My eternal thanks is due to Jesus Christ for being my way, truth, and life. I also want to appreciate Walter Alan Scott for his selfless, unwavering support. You ain't seen nothing yet! Thanks to my editor, Amber Keys, for embracing *Voice and Valor: An Autobiography for Re-humanization,* immediately and my brother Rodney Artis, whose God-given greatness is destined to take the world by storm.

Special thanks to everyone who read my excerpts and abided my enthusiasm to hear their feedback—it meant more to me than you know! I picked you because I knew you'd be honest.

Finally, I dedicate *Voice and Valor* not only to those who are re-humanizing but also to those who know they should. God's grace and mercy are waiting for you. Think for yourself and be integral; forgive yourself and others; apologize profusely and experience forgiveness from others on this side before you cross over. We can't control everything. Be healed within and be freed in the non-religious, authenticity of Jesus Christ!

Back cover photo by Nicholas Von Thrower, nicholasvonthrower@gmail.com.

About the Editor

Amber Bender was born and raised in Newville, Pennsylvania in the heart of Amish country. She is currently seeking a Bachelor of Arts in English Literature while perfecting her craft as an editor and author out of her home in Richmond, Virginia. She employs her experiences with good food and travel to write about the world through the eyes of its many fascinating peoples. Bender is the CEO of Piquant Publishing.

Voice and Valor

Foreword

"When writing the story of your life, don't let anyone else hold the pen." This quote is true, especially when someone is writing an autobiography or some literary piece detailing personal events that have occurred in the author's life. But, it can also mean taking control of one's life as seen in this book, *Voice and Valor*, an influential, expressive autobiographical narrative by Dante A. Payton, whom I have the pleasure and distinct honor of calling one of my closest friends. Being friends for over a decade, I met the author when he became a member of the church I attended in Norfolk, Virginia and he became a member of the choir of which I was a part. Not only did he have a wonderfully melodic and powerful tenor voice, but his personality and humor were equally harmonious. What struck me the most about him was his intelligence and devotion in doing the will of God. I found that he was extremely prophetic and knowledgeable of the Word of God and the deep mysteries surrounding His omnipotence. This led to many in depth conversations and from there a friendship developed based on mutual respect.

Not soon after, his gifts and talents led him to become the worship leader and head of the praise team. These were a select few who were not only great singers, but those who had an awareness in ushering in the presence of God. I was humbled to be selected to be in this group and it was here where

Voice and Valor

I found Dante to be adept at bringing out the talents and skills that lay dormant in each of us. What most surprised me was that he saw that I was could be a powerful expeditor in ushering in the presence of the Lord, a skill which I was not accustomed to. Dante presented me with a song, *Mighty God*, by the renown Shekinah Glory Ministries Choir, a song which was not in my comfort zone and I thought he had lost his mind. When I protested, he gently chided me and ensured me that I would do just fine and true to Holy Spirit, who guided Dante's choice, I did above and beyond what I had expected.

This and numerous other incidents led me to believe Dante was indeed a rare a gifted personality in the Kingdom. When I decided to write my own novel, *The Celestial Knights, the Advent of Go'El,* I sought him out to help me develop the numerous characters and the storyline that propelled this story into an epic narrative like the *Harry Potter* series, *The Lord of the Rings* saga, *The Chronicles of Narnia* and *The Chronicle of Brothers* account by Wendy Alec and even showed great skill by editing my book professionally. When he told me, he was going to write his book, I was intrigued because he had previously shown he had tremendous aptitude as a writer, having had me proofread some of his scholarly works he had prepared for the masters and doctorate programs he was in. I knew the Body of Christ as well as the world in general was in for a treat.

Voice and Valor

Reading his work, I was blown away by the rawness of his struggles and the magnitude of what most, if not all men go through in their assessment of what it means to be a man. Dante takes his reader on a journey through his life all the while teaching what it means to be a man, not through what society deems as manhood, but what it means in the eyes of the Lord. The modern world men are often portrayed as dense, selfish, arrogant, sexually immoral and at least potentially violent. A man who acts the way society thinks he should, particularly toward women, is often referred to as a "real man" or a "man's man." Sadly, this popular image of "real" manliness is based on misinformation and bad assumptions. God, the designer of human beings, sees things differently than society does. "Do not look at his appearance or at his physical stature ... For the Lord does not see as man sees; for man looks at the outward appearance, but the Lord looks at the heart" (1 Samuel 16:7). Looking at the heart is a concept lost on much of modern culture. It's much easier to use only what we see as the basis for our opinions and actions. Dante's book captures this concept poignantly as we see the hurt and pain he went through struggling with his own concepts of manhood and sexuality and his determination to be a "man after God's own heart." Dante showed me that in his brokenness, different in some ways, but similar in others, I saw my own shortcomings and how God wants spiritual brokenness, the kind of brokenness He can use. He wants godly sorrow that leads to repentance, not a condemnation for what we determine as sin, but for what God sees as sin. Not a specificity for a transgression, but for failing to follow what God has said. Dante once said to me, "The most wonderful thing about sin is that it makes you so desperate that all you want is God." Yes, deep sin can make us desperate. And out of that desperation, out of grief and the hurt of a fractured heart over sin, God longs to produce humility in us. It is humility that allows us to recognize, as Dante did, who God is and who we are in comparison with him. It is humility that sets us up to come to grips with our sin.

One of our conversations began with the validity of the Word of God. Now, before many of you Christians who are reading this begin to condemn me to the fiery pits of the Abyss, let me say, this, I believe that the Bible contains the unequivocal truth of God, inspired by Holy Spirit, yet, men wrote the Bible and translated its words. This introduced elements of personality, belief and political canon into its translations, especially in areas used to dominate and subjugate large portions of the populace. In its original Hebrew and Aramaic, there are words that were translated inaccurately and over the centuries these incorrect words became dogma and gave us an incorrect translation of what certain portions of the Scriptures God had intended. Some of these Scriptures involve the meaning of homosexuality, for example, the crime that was committed by the men of Sodom and Gomorrah was based on the treatment of strangers, instead of an outright condemnation of their wanting to "know" the three angelic strangers. This has led me on an exploration of passages that have been historically used to attack LGBTs, something we as Bible believers should not do. In my research, I found the chapter *Ambiguity* in John Polkinghorne's book, *Testing Scripture*, the quote, *"The tapestry of life is not colored in simple black and white, representing an unambiguous choice between the unequivocally bad and the unequivocally good. The ambiguity of human deeds and desires means that life includes many shades of grey. What is true of life in general is true also of the Bible in particular. An honest reading of Scripture will acknowledge the presence in its pages of various kinds of ambiguity."*

From reading Dante's autobiographic work and the numerous conversations, we have had, I can unapologetically say of my friend, he is truly a testament to the grace of God. When he divulged to me the most painful parts of his life, all I could say was I couldn't see why he wasn't a "stark-raving lunatic". All the hurt and misfortune he had experienced in his life would have driven a normal person insane, but God had, and has, a plan for Dante's life. Through my relationship with Dante, I found that sexuality is not all there is to an individual. We place too much emphasis on who a person is sleeping with, instead of looking at the qualities that make an individual unique. Dante is truly an exceptional person, gifted with a wonderful sense of humor, a kind heart and a dynamic intellect that spans a wide variety of disciplines. Though he is a gay man and I am not, I have no problem with saying, Dante is one of a few persons I can call not just a friend, but I embrace him as a brother.

Through my brotherhood with Dante, I began to see all people, regardless of their story, are deeply and unconditionally loved by God, each created with profound dignity and worth, not one more than another. This is more than mere religious happy talk [no matter where you stand on sin issues]— it is truth whether one is gay, bi sexual, asexual, or straight. Dante's book shows this is basic Christianity and the great equalizer of all people.

Minister R. A. Artis

Author, The Celestial Knights, the Advent of Go'El

Voice and Valor

Prologue

My autobiographical vignettes are not at all meant to be chronological, so they will not move from my birth-date forward. Plus, if I had attempted to start from conception, I would have bogged myself down and never completed the goal. These stories are formatted (narratively and sometimes non-grammatically, jumping to relevant connections in time) in a manner in which I hope you will hear my voice and still find its content entertaining, educational, transformative, and above all relatable.

In December 2016, I selected the bold, italicized headings from various sources and began writing the stories early Christmas morning. A number of family members and friends have read excerpts from the pages you're about to turn and found their own stories being told. Mine are metaphoric for anyone who's ever felt excluded or like an outcast and who is ever-embracing their personal journey. If you've ever come to think differently about those whom you've known all your life, then this book may be for you.

You too may liken yourself to an obscure group Jesus mentioned. He said, *And other sheep I have, which are not of this fold: them also I must bring, and they shall hear my voice; and there shall be one fold, and one shepherd (John 10:16, KJV).*

In writing this book, my simple aim is to tell my truth. I desire not to tear down anyone or any institution, religious or political; however, I aspire to stimulate thought in my readers. We need to re-humanize dehumanized individuals. Non-heterosexuals, for that matter, is one population of society that crosses the lines of hegemony — race, religion, sex, socioeconomic classes, etc. We are not always experiencing the full benefits of humanity due to ignorance, assumptions, and cruelty. As a passionate man of God, who happens to be bisexual, I felt it imperative to become an author. What better way than by first telling my own story?

Indeed, one of the blessings and curses of being an overcomer is having a long memory. My book will expose me — my personality, mentality (at various stages), and spirituality. No longer to remain a victim of other peoples' volitions, I am sharing my V's: the first being *Voice and Valor: An Autobiography for Re-humanization.*

Voice and Valor

Voice: A Right of Self-Expression

Voice and Valor

"A circle of trust has no agenda other than to support the inner journey of each person in the group, to make each soul feel safe enough to show up and speak its truth and to help each person listen to his or her inner teacher." (Parker J. Palmer)

Voice and Valor

"Are you gay?" This was the question my concerned fifty-year-old grandmother asked me as she held the heterosexual pornographic magazine I thought I'd cleverly hidden under my mattress. I was in the seventh grade. Embarrassed, guilty, and confused, I sat between her and her intensely silent oldest daughter, Sweet, whom I later painfully learned I'd mistrusted with my life. Looking back on this, I can see how *loaded* Sweet seemed.

Although I am very masculine now, my first twelve years on Earth had already revealed my tomgirlish fascination with femininity; men seemed dumb at that stage of my development because women won all the arguments. At age four I broke my leg after constantly disobeying my grandparents' orders to stop jumping off the front porch, playing Wonder Woman. A year later, Sweet railroaded me by setting up a surprise confrontation involving a neighboring three- or four-year-old White boy. She was sitting on the porch, seemingly bored and opportunistic, watching us. She suddenly asked my friend if he liked playing with me.

"Sometimes," he said.

I dropped my head. Sweet called us into the house and the bedroom she shared with her closest sister. We were told to sit on the bed, and she shut the door. Intelligent and frightened, I knew what was about to happen. Raised in a homophobic, Christian home my blood-aunt cast a condescending look at me but turned warmly toward my friend.

"Tell me Dante what he did to you and that you didn't like it."

I knew to say nothing. I cried. News soon hit our eleven-or-so member, two-story household that I had been kissing and belly-rubbing with a boy. We also rode big-wheels, wagons, go-carts, and climbed trees, laughed, and shot water guns at each other, but positive interactions, as I came to know, meant nothing when homosexual behavior was in question. I was mortified further when tearfully escorted to the boy's house to apologize to his father for what I'd done — double betrayed and scapegoated. We were not allowed to play together anymore. I was only five years old.

With all this in my background, Grandma found her son's adult magazine hiding where I slept. I responded to her inquiry with a shaky no, out of sheer ignorance and uncertainty as to what gay really meant. All I knew was what I was taught; that I'd be doomed to Hell and that it represented weakness. What child would have said yes at that age in those days? According to our faith system, society in the late 1980s, and what I discovered about taboos in the African-American culture, it wasn't in my best interest to own up to being the worst thing on earth. I felt utterly alone among people who loved me far more than I knew, yet were completely inept to support me.

Sweet was in her early thirties when she asserted, "You were looking at both the men and the women, but the homosexual spirit transferred itself to you as you were looking at it. If you keep this up, you will be living a double life."

What 7th grader deserves such intense, age-inappropriate counsel?

I kinda knew what Sweet was saying, but the condemnation of her word choice weighed on me, stirring mixed emotions of future and false guilt and the anger that accompanied feelings of abandonment. Truth is, I looked up to her and was sorely disappointed. Self-centered and self-impressed, Sweet bore an expression as if receiving a fresh download of revelation from Heaven. Grandma looked at her in shock. I didn't know what to say.

Sweet Painter had been building quite a reputation for herself as a woman of song, doctrine, and prayer. I am unaware as to whether or not she had yet embraced her prophetic calling, but her logic was indeed, senseless. She had an agenda — to build her own voice. Mine, however, was crumbling under the gravity of religious dogma, our family's strict code of obedience to elders, and now Sweet's spiritual influence at my expense. Grandma, whom I loved so dearly and wished had birthed me, was also afraid to disagree with "God."

I could later sense that Grandma felt as though Sweet overused her gifts. The answer to whether or not Grandma ever approached her about this, I may never know. Testimonies, however, of the accuracy of Sweet's prophetic prayers and gifts were mounting, no doubt swelling her naive head, making the thought of challenging her seem futile. Truth is, at that time, the Painter Family had very little understanding of the prophetic and how it can be used to manipulate and control others. To think for oneself was not taught in most Christian circles, especially in Black churches. Consequently, anyone claiming to speak on God's behalf was highly regarded even to the point that recipients would feel guilty for disagreeing with the messenger.

A future prophetic trainer would teach me the dangers of allowing one's gift(s) to become their identity. Indeed, people with low self-esteem and unchecked insecurities often find themselves drawn to this sense of power.

Still mystified by the interrogation, I repeated "no" but wrestled internally. Paranoia and shame poised themselves to split my mind. I highly respected Sweet's spirituality and Grandma's uncanny wisdom, but we were taught — rather *caught* — the notion to be afraid of our humanity. Insecure and desperately striving to please God, I was afraid that *that spirit* was trying to keep something from me. After all, I'd been told I have a heavy calling on my life and that the devil fights people like me the hardest.

My mind swirled with questions: *Was God unhappy with me? Am I* choosing *to be an abomination in God's sight?* — I know now, however, that no one *chooses* their sexuality. — *Do thoughts automatically equate to desire? How can I stop these thoughts? Would admitting to them inevitably subject me to some sort of frightening exorcism?* I imagined myself being forcibly laid hands upon by some strange minister as I cried, pleaded, and reached out for Grandma and Sweet, not because I didn't want to be "delivered" but because I was simply scared. I wanted to be *free*, but already knew I couldn't trust them. Circle of trust? Not for me. Inner teacher? He sounded condemning and angry.

Voice and Valor

I was still a growing and impressionable boy. Looking back on my natural curiosities about sex and pornography, I was neither focusing specifically on the male genitalia in the magazine nor the female, fully-exposed centerfold models. I was genuinely fascinated by both roles long before I understood why.

I hadn't had any real experiential knowledge as to what to do with my penis. Even though I sort of knew what men did with it, I was too young to own any sexuality. Yet, I understood that I'd *better* say I liked girls. Developmentally, I wasn't there; the only guys that liked girls were "humping" them, as we called it, but I couldn't tell my grandma and Sweet that! The confrontation made me feel as though I made some damning decision to be curious, not to mention gay. The most I did at twelve was grind, or "dry hump" pillows, pretending it was my girlfriend similar to all boys my age. Mothers/women don't know what it's like to have a penis and are often ignorant as to how to intelligently address their son's sexuality no matter his orientation.

Indeed, Sweet's line of questioning violated some major boundary and was, therefore, extremely unfair and unnecessary. She, a victim of misogyny (in her own right), was also using me to practice her gift (more like witchcraft) thereby inflating herself with spiritual pride. Whenever Sweet would feel the need to "stand as a prophet," the woman often came off *soulish*, or "in her flesh," as Christians would say. Her inner and spoken voice would proclaim, "Since I said it, it is so!"

That common belief is dangerously false, damaging, anti-Christ, and typical of tyrants. While some people take pleasure in instilling fear, thinking harder degrees of rebuke make you more or less prescient. Those who like to rebuke others don't like it when it's their turn to receive it. I learned from future spiritual gifts and trainings that the overarching spirit (or aim) of healthy prophecy is to edify (build up), to exhort (stir up), and to comfort (cheer up). Spiritual abusers do the opposite, which is to embarrass, expose, and control others. Prophecy is what Jesus would say. One day I believe God will look many of us eye-to-eye and ask, "What did you say *I* said?"

The same Sweet would still later become my confidante and third mother, whom I respected above Mother Free-Spirit who bore me but not as much as I revered Grandma. This singular dysfunction is the prevailing obstacle which God is using to shape my passions for His glory. He has seen me through times when Sweet feigned support and trust but told my secrets to anyone she befriended. Whenever self-condemnation defeated me growing up, Sweet told me my "past was under the blood of Jesus Christ." (Translation: *Move past it because God has forgotten it, so do not define yourself according to your past sins.*) However, Sweet told anyone, especially if they were spiritual. Barbara Coloroso, author of *The Bully, the Bullied, and the Bystander,* said that people like Sweet are devious and manipulative; she can act as if she is a caring and compassionate person, but it is only a guise to get what she wants. Social bullies, according to Coloroso, are jealous of your positive qualities and use gossip and rumors to socially exclude you. And, even though they may be popular, they are not someone other people would want to confide in, lest they too become a target.

Once I returned from college, I began to distance myself from Sweet. I no longer told her every step I took and had chosen "to grow my own brain and balls," as I commonly say. This loss of control made her angry with me though she would most likely never admit it. Unable to let go and allow me to be my own man, Sweet sought a means to keep tabs. I imagined my ex-wife, Lady O, secretly told Sweet that I was physically abusing her. Fueled with the notion that she "knew" me,

Voice and Valor

Sweet believed Lady O and told the spouse about my "past struggles" with homosexuality. Notably, I'd had no same-sex encounter in years. I was "walking out my deliverance" as instructed before I decided to marry. I had neither an anger problem nor history of violence with anyone (male or female). However, Sweet didn't know that Lady O was a habitual liar before siding with her. My blood relative forfeited her right to be a part of my circle of trust when she villainized me and told fellow church members that I beat my wife because I really wanted a man.

Voice and Valor

"It will be a sign of maturity or of immaturity whether one perceives or fails to perceive from this experience that what confronts us here is not the stubborn and narrow-minded self-complacency of old age or its fear of allowing youth to assert itself, but it is a question of the safeguarding or the violation of an essential ethical law" (Dietrich Bonhoeffer)

Voice and Valor

As with many families, the Painters suffer from a condition which I refer to as *the pride of the elders*. Sweet's youngest brother, Jew, loved chiming "children should be seen and not heard" when I was a minor, despite the fact that he was just under ten years older than me. This is an old-school notion, no doubt one which was passed down to him growing up. I speculate that he said this to other peoples' kids and that it was even more awkward, equally demeaning, and just as unappreciated. While children need to be taught boundaries, they should never be mistreated simply for being youngsters. This devaluing mindset originated long before Jew; a generational curse that stole the voices of so many of my family members. Moreover, too many of us seek to be heard through gossiping about one another.

Sociologists define *significant others* as those who have the ability to influence your emotions and sense of well-being. To my folks, age was a badge, and being older automatically meant one was more mature than their juniors. After all, with age came wisdom — another false adage. I once read Paulo Freire's *Pedagogy of the Oppressed* where he noticed that oppressed individuals tend to envy their oppressors, seeing the oppressors as "adults." They saw their oppressors' position as a way out of their plight and could not wait until the day when they would become oppressors themselves. No wonder the cycle perpetuates for so long in the Painters. We are over-spiritual, unrealistic, and unethical.

Additionally, the concept of respect, for example, was perverted and used as an arbitrary means to "freeze" or keep younger ones "stuck" and "in their place." This usually happened when a youth's reasoning was perceived as a threat to an older person's agenda. Many of my relatives also struggled with anxiety and comforted themselves by attempting to upstage each other in front of company. We craved power. The way to get it was by way of age, status, and gossip. I had to unlearn this behavior.

Fear is akin to traditionalism. I believe many of you, my adult readers, can attest to how those who "knew you when" desire to treat you as if you're still sixteen years old. Abusive elders fear letting go of what they knew about you and are apprehensive about what you are becoming. A fellow author and good friend told me that one.

Cousin Smooth, in his mid-thirties, while commenting on this passage said he had to distance himself from certain family members because they made him feel like a child. Why do too many loved ones treat outsiders like royalty and disrespect insiders, and then when the consequences of those actions take effect, they pretend that we should all still be close-knit? Some of you may have children of your own, rent or own your home, or even possess a voter registration card, but your older loved ones are overly-parental, overly involving themselves in your adult life.

Genuine advice is one thing, but vicarious motives are something different. Such "elder" behavior is immature and unethical. Parents should learn how to treat their adult-children. No adult should be treated like the kid they once were. This constitutes an abuse and over-extension of parental authority. Can I get an amen?

One should never confuse wisdom with their personal comfort zone.

A recent conversation with a close friend confirmed the way many junior individuals behave around their seniors. Respectful, good-natured younger ones purposely dumb ourselves down so as to make room/show respect for the sage advice, input, and reasoning from those who've preceded us. We've admitted openly and without question giving elders the floor. Too many (NOT ALL) seniors become prideful, abuse their "authority," and overstep their boundaries via their tone, untimeliness, expressions, or actions. They soon feel compelled to take the lead in younger adult affairs. When is it ever appropriate for a grandparent to correct the parent in front of the grandkids? Never. This is when the euphemized "advice" becomes overbearing and pressuring. Indeed, with pride comes presumption (behavior perceived as arrogant, disrespectful, and transgressing the limits of what is permitted or appropriate). Seniors shouldn't speak to younger adults in a manner which says *do what I say* and/or *do it my way*. Adult juniors want the same regard seniors wanted from their own elders.

Respect goes both ways, but abusive seniors don't like admitting they've disrespected us. Entitlement shouldn't come with age either, especially when abuses (mostly verbal) are in question. Does anyone else find something wrong with normalizing senior citizens to say/do whatever they want simply because they've been on Earth longer? In my opinion, members from such an advanced age group, if no one else, should be the most experienced in exemplifying kindness and respect. However, we've normalized ornery behavior. Outside of cases of genuine dementia or

Voice and Valor

Alzheimer's, there should be no excuse for rudeness. Personally, if I was nearing the end of my life, I'd want to be mindful of how I treated others, considering the fact that I can't correct my wrongs once this life is over.

When we think about it, each new generation is the progression from the one which preceded it. Indeed, there is a gap between the old school and new school. If only we could get representatives from both groups in one room to respectfully dialogue because, as I see it, I believe the old school thinks the new school is out of control, and the new school thinks the old school had too much control. Because we could never be God, there will always be something for us to learn from each other.

A friend once told me the fastest way to get old is to stop learning.

I can readily identify with a conscious preacher who said that we should be thinking about what we're thinking about. Embracing this, I began validating my feelings about my or other peoples' observations of "the stubborn and narrow-minded self-complacency of old age." I had pondered this and held it in the back of my mind for some time and found camaraderie with a much older scholarly stranger, Mr. Bonhoeffer. Ironically, he was writing to oppressive German, religious authorities back some time in the mid-20th century. This is one of the reasons I am such an advocate for lifelong learning. Without my having pursued higher education, I doubt I would have been able to academically bolster my thinking because of my surroundings. He too must have known the feeling of being "surrounded by idiots." Have you ever asked yourself "is it just me or…?"

Do not get me wrong. I don't think myself better than anyone, family or outsider. It's just that having humbled myself to healthy mentorship, reading transformative material, and developing my own "self-maintenance kit" (being integral about the strengths and weaknesses of my behavior and knowing how to check myself) has expanded my mind. What breaks my heart is when people I know refuse to want better for themselves.

Furthermore, they even choose to speak to me as if everything they know should mean the world to me. Some time in my mid-thirties, I remember when Spicy sternly approached me about a writing that was published in an online newsletter. Its owner was one of my former pastors whose ministry Spicy had previously suggested to me. Knowing her combative temperament and how she bounces everything off Sweet, I ignored Spicy's tone. It is duly noted that the pair thought of themselves as the deciding judges, jurors, and executioners in nearly everything simply because they were the oldest of their mother's children. They were so close that you'd think they were twins. I calmly asked Spicy how she found out about it. She frowned as she told me one of the church elders (where Sweet pastors) showed it to them.

"You just be doing stuff!" Spicy scolded. She was angry because I didn't ask her permission as if even a 20-year-old needed her approval to do anything, let alone something this positive. She and her sister practiced what I call *false authority*.

Even though I shook my head at her internally, I maintained my composure. She and her sister took her rank as "aunt" way too seriously. But not even Solomon could abide contentious women.

"I'm glad you read it."

Spicy remained visibly dissatisfied that I didn't repent to her for my decision. I could tell the pair were using each other to keep tabs on me. Also, I presume that my gentle response disarmed her as she sat glaring. I walked away from her, eager to avoid further scrutiny. This is one of the instances where Sweet would have accused me saying, "His age has gone to his head." Sadly, they failed to realize that they were guilty of their own accusation.

It is so true that God cannot be mocked. I'll never forget the Saturday morning one of their uncles (my grand-uncle) made his usual grand visit to the Painter Family house with a huge surprise. The living room door was wide open. With scarcely a knock, he flung the screen door and marched to Sweet's and Spicy's bedroom, stuttering as he spoke. Uncle Juniper abruptly asked the duo if they were gay. In his mind since they were over thirty, always together, and unmarried they had to have been lesbians. He was their elder, and they knew to mind their tone when addressing his accusations, no matter his approach. You should have heard Spicy's vehemence and Sweet's more silent but equal contempt after he left. Boundaries were, indeed, violated. However, could this have been an example of the biblical law of sowing and reaping, "karma," as the world calls it? Do you think they connected this rude encounter with their uncle with how they treated me? Better believe they didn't and haven't.

Grasping the irony of this encounter with overbearing Spicy and Sweet, I reflected on the revelation God allowed me to share in the newsletter.

The Lord had asked me, "Dante, what does it mean to truly love someone?"

I was mature enough in my walk with God to know He was referring to *agape* — unconditional love (and not the brotherly or romantic type). I also knew that if He asks us questions, then He already knows the answers. So, I smirked.

"Lord, what do *You* believe it means to truly love someone?"

I heard His mind smile and say, "I'm glad you asked." The volume of God's response reverted to the timbre of His original inquiry when He said, "You know you love someone when you see how much your own weaknesses affect them, and you care enough to change."

Now, if that blessed you, Reader, just imagine if I had sought my elders' approval and then my aunts had advised me not to share it with the world?

Sweet and Spicy in particular, claimed to love me, but whenever my independence somehow threatened their co-dependent thinking, they exhibited unloving tendencies as if I was somehow exempt from kindness and respect. I was aware of it and knew they were not, but wouldn't have been "heard" had I said it.

Self-reflection is critical to maturation and development. Sadly, many people who are blood-related to the Painters have failed to allow Holy Spirit to check them. It never seems to amaze me how so many of us know Jesus is the life, yet we fail to apply this knowledge to our own lives. The love of God is kind, but we are uncomfortable being nice and mutually respectful. We neglect certain family members' signs of discomfort while treating outsiders like royalty. This sounds more like we have a religion (an external, hypocritical form of godlikeness) instead of a genuine relationship with God (an expanding inward rule of Holy Spirit). Since we claim to love Jesus and want to be like Him, then we should be producing evidence of love, joy, peace, patience, kindness, gentleness, goodness, faithfulness, and self-control. Galatians 5 tells us there is no penalty for operating in these fruits. Is it a wonder Buddhist monks exhibit an inner peace that models that which Christians preach and rarely attain?

Sweet and Spicy, as with many of us, were victims of "the pride of the elders." They learned this from their no-nonsense, old-school father and compatibly milder authoritarian mother who learned it from their predecessors. The generations instilled a *respect-your-elders* type of approach for youngsters which generally meant do whatever an adult tells you without question, backtalk, or defiant expression.

I got "beatings," as Black folks call it, not beat-downs. There's a difference between corporal discipline and genuine abuse, Scary People! I was issued consequences that taught me to respect authority and helped me to become an overall great person. Reflecting on a lot of children today, I would never have gotten away with a smidgen of what they did or said. Body language was essential when I grew up, too. This meant that if you dared to signify that you had "an opinion," you doomed yourself to a backhand. Did anyone else just hear Chris Tucker say, "Damn! You just got knocked the fuck out!" (pardon the language, but this candid writing will be just that)? The rationale in our families was to spank them as they grow, so that the police won't have to do far worse when their grown. Home-training was also a means to instill within us a sense of self-awareness and self-respect so as not to embarrass ourselves and/or our parents. Moreover, disrespectful behavior by minors was taken personally by their guardians.

As an aside: Parents need to parent so that

teachers can teach.

The darker side of this "pride of the elders" coincides with Bonhoeffer's mention of the fear of youthful expression. Grandad, for example, was very impatient with listening to us youngsters. His rough hands were hardly far from the conversation — well, command. Being reared in such an overly-strict environment passed on to Mother Free-Spirit and her siblings to the point where they struggled during much of their lives with respecting each others' voices. No wonder they tried to pass this onto their children, with the exception of Sweet, Sharon, and Sal. Nevertheless toxic shame, as defined by John Bradshaw, necessitates us to cope with its infliction, usually in a destructive manner.

The aforementioned relative, Uncle Jew, informed me that a number of the Painter Family once assembled to view the remains of the last car Grandma was in before she died. I asked him why hadn't anyone called me to the meeting.

He said, "You wouldn't have wanted to see it."

In disbelief, I asserted, "Yes, I would have."

His *uncle-ship* must have made him counter, "No! You wouldn't have been able to handle it!"

Voice and Valor

I was speechless as I took in this crazy phone conversation. Whether or not this was a cover up for excluding me, he presumed to speak for me as if I would have lost my mind and been rendered completely inconsolable at the sight of the totaled vehicle. The Painters were no strangers to mellow drama either, by the way. The last I remembered was Jew crying on my shoulder when I arrived home telling me that Grandma, his mother, had died. I had driven almost two hours from college after receiving the news. Jew must have seen me arrive and park on the side of the house under our pine tree. He greeted me, understandably teary-eyed and somber. I patted him on the back calmly saying, "I know." Jew reacted with a sudden contempt that I wasn't as emotional as he was, grunted, and walked away. I was hurting that Wednesday just like everyone else. What he didn't know about me was that, in times of crisis, I have a short, intense emotional response. However, I can very quickly compose myself to tend to others. Once everyone is safe and things are settled, I then succumb to my emotions.

Three years before this writing, Jew, in a much later conversation, revealed to me that he felt his older sisters took his voice as well. I empathized with him, and listened to his story. I was accustomed to being cut off by him at the slightest indication of youthful expression; therefore, I was surprised Jew afforded me the chance to share how I felt he had done the same to me. He indulged me in a light discussion of famed psychologist Alfred Adler's "birth order" concept. I good-naturedly told him I believed he felt I dethroned him as "the baby of the family" when his parents were awarded physical custody of me. He apologized. We developed a better relationship over the next couple months.

However, at the writing of this book, Jew and I haven't spoken in over a year. Never mind the fact that I had paid him a triple financial kindness to him and his girlfriend just weeks prior. Spiritualizing his inability to repay me, Jew asserted that Jehovah would bless me abundantly. Still, I knew he harbored prejudice against me about my sexuality, although I hadn't yet fully accepted it myself.Our differences were on the eternal implications of President Obama's favor of the Supreme Court's decision to legalize gay marriage. Radical Christians would do well to learn that on Election Day, we're not voting for a pastor and that the founders of the United States of America were Deists, not necessarily *Christians*.

Some would argue that most of us and our

Voice and Valor

Christian elders follow Paul more closely than they do Christ Himself.

Voice and Valor

"Whether [memories] and stories of past events focus on matters of sex, there are often additional implicit and nonverbal clues and messages about sexuality and homosexuality that they have carried to adulthood" (Betty Berzon and Robert Leighton)

Voice and Valor

Similar to the glass ceiling other marginalized groups experienced, I realize that I suffered most of my life from a failure to spiritually climax. This was largely due to "toxic shame" (John Bradshaw). Dr. N. Cindy Trimm and Bradshaw would agree that "shame" is an internal feeling that we are somehow flawed as a person. Trimm wrote, "It seduces people into believing that they are inadequate, bad, and no good. These feelings impede the maximization of potential and the fulfillment of purpose. In some people, it can result in low self-esteem and a poor concept of self."

My upbringing consisted of the lack of exclusive biological parental guidance, a confusing relationship with Mother Free Spirit, the overruling yet fit voices of maternal grandparents, and Sweet's overbearing spiritual influence and encouragement of her new friends to "speak" into my life. The ministers would nickname it, I believe, in a simultaneous attempt to appease Sweet and to protect my dignity. I wasn't stupid, but felt obligated to endure Sweet's obsessions with the gifts of the spirit and sexuality. Knowing the stigma associated with same-sex attraction and of Sweet's gossipy ways, my personal business could never be my own. My boundaries were violated continually. I couldn't resist becoming paranoid, having been made to believe I was more effeminate than I actually was as I matured. The Good News Translation of Proverbs 29:25 states, *It is dangerous to be concerned with what others think of you, but if you trust the Lord, you are safe.* Multiple predicaments such as these instilled a subconscious over-concern of what others thought of me. Virtually, everyone's opinion dictated how I felt about myself; this is why finding my voice was so delayed.

According to Dr. Betty Berzon, "The roots of some [non-heterosexuals'] present attitudes and feelings toward the Church — both positive and negative — can be found in [religious] teachings or experiences with [Christian] authority figures including their own parents and family, teaching ministers, [and peers]." We all are familiar with the scriptures used to condemn homosexuality. But the bad treatment and over-emphasis is what non-heterosexuals oppose most. This is what is going "unheard."

While in my twenties, I had privately confessed my struggles with same-sex attraction to a pastor. The following Sunday's sermon topic was "homosexuality in the church." I remember feeling betrayed and increasingly uncomfortable. I knew I should have taken my friend's advice and not told the man of God for this very reason; he called me up at the end of his message, embraced me, and burst into tears as he pulled me down with him and sat on the altar steps, rocking back and forth. One can't be "delivered" while experiencing humiliation at the same time. What would these onlookers think of me after the benediction? I wasn't ready to verbalize any of my personal affairs. The shame, judgment, and condemnation I felt delayed my coming into my own truth.

You could only imagine my surprise when later in life I discovered I Thessalonians 4:7, NIV, which said, *And to make it your ambition to lead a quiet life: You should mind your own business and work with your hands, just as we told you...* No wonder preaching this to someone can be so powerful.

On a much lighter biographical note, I'll never forget a hilarious "sex education" session. I may have been in middle school then. Smooth and I recalled in jest the time one of our uncles staged a serious impromptu talk. It bears noting that I believe his actions were most likely instigated by Sweet because he naturally would have left this up to his dad, our grandfather. Needless to say, we were annoyed from being summoned from the television but sat on the bed and gave him our attention. When he referred to the female genitalia as her "pa-pajyna-pajyna" (yes, he stuttered a bit), we raised our eyebrows, glanced at each other briefly, and held in our laughter. We knew we'd be in trouble if we so much as made anything but a straight face at the elder. I think he instinctively knew he mispronounced it, however, he would not suffer correction from kids. We love Uncle Muscle. He has a learning disability, but he was our protector.

One night, Muscle caught me and another boy masturbating on the side of the house. Muscle remained in silent agreement as his younger brother Jew, both homophobic and misinformed, told me that the act of "playing with myself" would turn me gay. This created a disturbing inner conflict. Imagine being around my male peers in college and the question as to whether I masturbated arose. I was ingratiated when an overzealous dorm floor-mate exclaimed, "I do on the regular!" Everyone burst with laughter. I snickered with a mix of relief, newfound clarity, and frustration at my uncles' advice.

In addition, being intelligent as a boy targeted me for shaming and often caused them to desire to treat me unfairly. My memories include a heavily intoxicated (possibly high) Pierre bursting through the back door and smacking my two younger cousins on the head and slapping mine against the refrigerator handle. All three of us cried. His girth, the alcoholic stench, his booming voice, and recurring violent energy brought us abject terror. Frightened and angry themselves, Sweet and Spicy got into a shouting match with their younger brother as they ran to their children's aid. When I looked up at Spicy for comfort, she side-eyed me. Full of contempt, the sister growled.

"What are you crying for?!"

The message I heard was "Stop crying like a little punk and be a man!" I was left with no one to console me. My mother was out in the streets and father absent. My terrifyingly unpredictable uncle was still within five feet away from me as a frightened and confused Dante was forced to suck up his sorrow, witness his cousins being protected, and wait in agony to bypass his aunts and cousins to desperately search for Grandma. Spicy's words had hit their mark. I was embarrassed but not allowed to complain.

Thankfully, the busted door and Sweet's and Spicy's yelling had alerted Grandad and Muscle to go after Pierre. The arguing told them Pierre had put his drunken hands on us kids. Their pursuit in the opposite direction brought me some comfort. Again, why was I wrong for being upset? Was I wrong for needing love?

It was as if the sound of my voice and seeing my tears irritated them. Holy Spirit reminded me while editing this section about a prophetic word telling me God gifted me with all the verbal gifts. Interestingly enough, this explains so much. I was always smart, and they readily dismissed me as a smart aleck when they said something that struck me as… *whaaa--?*. In truth, I was a sneaky kid and a typical bully but a kid, nonetheless. Unfortunately, I doubt some of my younger cousins know how much I dearly love them. Many of them seem to be "stuck" in the past, not realizing I'm not the same "jerk" I used to be growing up. Some of their perceptions are a product of taking up someone else's offenses or simply *plural ignorance*. Years before this writing, I had genuinely put away childish things, but what can you do when people don't want to heal from the past and/or get to know the present you? Yet, I was truly a "good boy" overall, very mannerly, jovial, talkative, and wanted to love God with everything.

Remarkably, it wasn't until my mid-thirties that I pondered the paradox a cerebral kid feels when s/he realizes s/he was raised by loved ones with learning disabilities and/or personality disorders. I recently learned in a summer 2017 certified nursing aide training class that a symptom of borderline personality disorder is an intense and stormy relationship with loved ones, family, and friends. Sweet, in particular, has extremes from love and closeness to dislike and anger. However, she would categorize her emotional shifts in attitude/opinion of loved ones, including those she has befriended, as signs of the prophetic. Ignorance comes in many different forms.

Thankfully, hard-working Grandad often boomed "get your lesson done" into our young ears. Further evidence of the dichotomy of shame was evidential when I was raised to do well in school but wasn't celebrated (at least by male family members) for it. I wasn't allowed to articulate as though I learned proper grammar. Jew, whom I looked up to most chiefly because he was the handsomest, sang well, and, although corny, made us all laugh. He unfortunately heckled me often for being intelligent, taunted me and called me names such as nerd and Brainiac while Muscle chuckled. You could only imagine the repressed anger I felt when watching a Saturday morning episode of the *Superfriends* with my uncles when the DC comics villain, Brainiac, appeared and, of course, Wonder

Voice and Valor

Woman. They glanced and smirked at me. All I could do was feel my humiliation and wish they were my size and weight so I could stand up to them and be heard. I wished I didn't stutter so badly; they were certain to mock me if I attempted to defend myself.

Instead, I gave in to self-hated and winced internally at each mention of the criminal's name. They were essential to my impression that I was not only unacceptable and White-sounding but also unmanly. Because of this, I struggled with self-authentication and speaking up, even against bad leadership advice due to the conditioned false belief that I was being disrespectful, weird, and wrong for doing so. It goes without saying, but I never would have used Jew's having dropped out of high school against him even if he loved making comments on my braininess and masculinity. Still, he told me that since I hadn't had my first fight by that young age, then that alone constituted a fundamental lack of a man's rite of passage. If "becoming a man" was a man's rite, what would he have called having dropped out of high school diploma and continually struggling to obtain his GED? Despite Jew's attitude, I would have loved to tutor him in mathematics, the part that haunts him most.

Going back to the Lord's permission to

spiritually advance in ministry, I recognized that I had always come close to the point of fulfillment, affirmation, or full acceptance, but… — there was always a "but" from hyper-masculine Christians (leaders and laity), judgmental women, or my self-debilitating inner voice, largely due to reservations about my sexuality. Nothing in the Bible or Christianity justifies discriminatory attitudes or prejudicial actions toward homosexuals. However, this singular difference is a largely unwelcomed characteristic despite the sincerity of our worship, personality traits, anointed ministry and/or faithful service. I remember numerous encounters with the glass ceiling when considered for ministerial licensure, ordination, and other promotions once suspicions of my "past" circulated. This "past" always mattered way too much, never allowing me to outlive it. It was carried and assumed as if it was my "present." Who could go back to undo his/her history? I've even been told by a Christian that my inability to attain financial breakthrough was due to my "struggle" with homosexuality.

Today (2017), I live in a world where discrimination against non-heterosexuals is identified as a form of bigotry. However, homophobia in the African-American community is typically stronger, and this is primarily the fault of non-thinking (religious) Church leaders. I courageously decided that God is disappointed at those who claim to love unconditionally but view same-sex-loving individuals as a condition.

Many Believers say God is love and that He loves through us, yet we are afraid to admit we don't behave lovingly toward everyone. Love is patient, kind, unselfish, not easily provoked, and more. Being a product of my upbringing, I am just recently finding my voice and adding it to this world. I am a born leader, and I can feel this God-given mandate accelerating its requirements on my life. I know I am not alone. It is almost a well-kept secret that some areas of the church world are helping gays and lesbians (and parents of) to reconcile sexuality and faith.

Voice and Valor

"The orientation is a deep-seated, relatively stable dimension of the personality usually experienced as a 'given' and not freely chosen" (Berzon and Leighton)

Voice and Valor

As a typical Christian, I was over-taught to be sin-conscious, giving partiality to sins of the flesh, including the notions of perversions, adultery, strange flesh, abominations (overemphasis on homosexuality), fornication, whoredom, and the lust of the flesh. Basic distinctions among sexual attraction, sexual orientation, sexual identity, and sexual conduct, on the other hand, are sternly avoided as if faith and science do not complement each other. Yet, while in the Old Testament, Daniel is known as a major prophet, interpreter of dreams, and intercessor, he was also characterized as good-looking, highly intelligent, a scientist, philosopher, and gifted linguist, allowing him the ability to master several different languages. Daniel's uniqueness validates the need for Christians, especially, to be smart and spiritual. Still, at face value, the wording of King James' Judeo/Christian language and American homophobia render discussions of sexuality as unnecessary and defiant against God. "You weren't *born* that way so get *born again*" and "God doesn't make *mistakes*" are common sayings used to debate against people who are thought to be non-heterosexual. People need to be re-educated.

The ancient council members who canonized Holy Bible had no knowledge of embryonic development; science was far less advanced then. Yet, even now, you don't know what you don't know. But… homosexuality wasn't thought of the way we think about it today. Reasons like these and so many more are reasons why everyone needs to love learning and to not avoid books because, in our ignorance, we end up targeting and harming innocent people. Even Jesus briefly affirmed the existence of eunuchs. We would most likely consider them asexuals. His mention signified He had more He could have offered, but the religious teachers (Pharisees, etc.) of His day couldn't have handled it. They privately quibbled over the Judeo-Christian laws but presented a hypocritical front in public.

We have a lot of modern-day Pharisees among us. These would be the ones holding and/or throwing rocks at society's outcasts…even in Jesus's name. The four gospels' depiction of Christ was one who welcomed sinners and transformed people's lives. He often talked about His relationship with His Heavenly Father. Jesus was not religious.

Special note: Reader, bear in mind that my usage of "religion/religious/religiosity" (pertaining to a system of beliefs, principles, creeds, dogma, and faith to which an individual adheres) is negative as it is the twin of tradition (elements of a culture passed down from generation to generation, especially by oral communication and modeling, usually forced and confining). While these may seem harmless, these forms of Godliness fuel spiritual pride and anxieties that are, in fact, hindrances to fresh moves of Holy Spirit. Citizens of the kingdom of God and heaven are relationship-oriented, where we know our God intimately and do exploits. Therefore, it is possible to be "religious" about someone/thing out of habit — no real passion, no real intimacy.

Most of us have heard of intersex individuals (formerly called hermaphrodites), ones born with a penis and a vagina. What about those whose sexuality isn't as physically apparent? Biologists confirm that every human being has varying proportions of estrogen and testosterone, which feminize and masculinize the brain and body, respectively. What happens when this process isn't as complete as *we* would prefer? I met a guy whose abusive mother felt enormous guilt for tormenting him before the doctor revealed his hormone levels registered 50% testosterone and 50% estrogen.

Psalm 139:15-16 (MSG) reads:

> *Oh yes, you shaped me first*
> *inside, then out; you formed me*

Voice and Valor

in my mother's womb. I thank
you, High God — you're
breathtaking! Body and soul, I
am marvelously made! I
worship in adoration — what a
creation! You know me inside
and out, you know every bone in
my body; You know exactly how
I was made, bit by bit, how I
was sculpted from nothing into
something. Like an open book,
you watched me grow from
conception to birth; all the
stages of my life were spread
out before you. The days of my
life all prepared before I'd even
lived one day.

Obviously, no one can control their physiology. Even while preparing to have this edited in June 2018, I was served by a very pleasant, soft-spoken female fast food employee. Her urban-masculine aura (even in uniform) suggested she was lesbian, despite her "girly" hairstyle. However, one could not deny her prominent, well-trimmed, stylized beard. No doubt her genetics required her to develop tough skin and a strong mind. Sexuality is chromosomal, not an alternate lifestyle or demon.

Voice and Valor

Bearing all this in mind, would God consider these two individuals as mistakes? Did heterosexuals "choose" to be "straight" or to produce queer offspring? Most of us are unaware of what it's like to be gay but have so much to say about those who are not heterosexual. Who would "choose" a life that would invite anger, cruelty, discrimination, ridicule, and, in some cases violence?

Mixed with water and bleach, Mother Free-Spirit once bathed me in the downstairs Painter Family bathtub. I was about eight or nine years old when she told me to lay first on my back and then turn over on my stomach. Seconds after my penis was submerged, I screamed to the top of my lungs. Frantic and burning, I must have tried to leap out because Free-Spirit attempted to shush me repeatedly. Grandma burst into the bathroom, demanding to know what was going on. I was confused and distraught.

"It burns!" I told her through tears.

Looking down at the weird water, I wondered why this bath felt so different from all the others. *It wasn't stinging my feet and lower shins,* I thought. Grandma grabbed a towel and rushed me to Free-Spirit's nearby bedroom, comforted me, and covered me in a sheet. Still unaware as to what happened, we looked into each other's eyes as I whimpered. No one made me feel safe like Grandma and the pain had already subsided by the time she left and returned. She asked me if she could examine me. I appeared fine as she kissed my tears away. Thirty years later, a conversation with Cousin Blessed revealed that Free-Spirit was trying to "cleanse" me that day.

Speaking to the aforementioned quote's note on personality, my temperament blend is more similar to the biblical David (as identified by the late Dr. Tom LaHaye's studies of Hippocrates' humors). I am predominantly an extreme extrovert (sanguine) and secondary mild introvert (melancholy), a SanMel. King David, too, was weak-willed, highly emotional, exhibited a flair for the arts, attracted men and women, bright, self-pitying, and among other things, had a tremendous capacity to commune with God. His profile makes him easily envied as well. Moreover, the depth of his relationships with Jonathan, King Saul, and Michal have been debated. David was/is still "a man after God's own heart."

From the Myers-Briggs standpoint, I also rank among 2% of the human population as a natural leader "Protagonist" (ENFJ); I am extroverted (opposite introvert), intuitive (not sensing), feeling (vs. thinking), and judging (as opposed to perceiving). There are numerous free online personality tests out there, by the way, and I encourage my readers to discover theirs. For those who prefer the DISC typography, the King and I are the equivalent of the "Influencer" and "Conscientious" combination. In life, David was rejected by his rough and tumble older brothers and father as a youth, but the horribly underestimated shepherd boy was destined to be one of history's greatest warriors.

Still, can you imagine David dancing around, singing, and playing the harp while tending his father's small flock of sheep? I am energetic and a very capable flutist and singer. These attributes classified me as "soft," especially growing up. Arrogant Eliab and his brothers didn't know David had fought a hungry lion and tiger, saved sheep, and bested the wild animals right under their noses. Conversely, I'm currently managing the constant, disrespectful, and inconvenient quips from blood-thirsty bigots. Once you're rumored to be a non-heterosexual man, straight guys are anxious around you, always wondering who's thinking they're gay too, or if you want them as well. Life is constantly teaching me to never allow people to speak for/on me, especially since they tend to like building their own reputation at my expense.

In my later thirties, I reunited with Jeffrey, who confessed to me that he was utterly amazed when seeing a "very masculine and anointed" young man leading praise and worship. Because of our mutual respect for one another, we shared a laugh when he said he'd believed I was going to be a "flamer" (a derogatory term usually referring to flamboyant gay men). Jeffrey and his family had come to live with the Painters while I was a boy, and he refreshed my memory of how Free-Spirit was always fussing at me. He (and other family members) routinely told her to stop being so mean to me. Apparently, everything I did came across as "gay" to Free-Spirit. Jeffrey was a trusted friend of ours, also "struggled" with homosexuality, was married to a doting wife (who knew his story), and had two children at the time (contrary to popular belief, not all non-heterosexuals are pedophiles!). This man always treated me with the utmost respect and provided me the absolute best Christmas I'd ever had! Jeff told me that Mother Free-Spirit knew about his issue and often confided in him about her fears that I'd become gay. I was, apparently, so effeminate to the point that it drove her to distraction. Insight allows me to ascertain that I must have caused her a great deal of shame as well. Very few women could have endured the grief of everyone knowing her "man-child" had broken his leg pretending to be Wonder Woman. How much taunting did she experience because of me? What were people saying about her?

Ironically, while enrolling in the sixth grade beginning band, Mother Free-Spirit sneakily ushered me into the back part of the Painter house into the kitchen (away from the earshot of her parents). She pressured me into playing the flute, ignoring the harassment I was destined to endure since it was still considered a girl's instrument in the 1980's. I told her I wanted to sign up for the saxophone. The public school system I grew up in had strongly advised parents to avoid picking instruments that could potentially damage a child's mouth; I had braces. Mother Free-Spirit's imbalance caused her to argue.

"Dante, there are a lot of professional men who play the flute."

Mother Free-Spirit hated the fact that I might by gay, right?

Credulous, I pleaded with her.

"People are going to joke me all my life, all

those years before I become famous."

In hindsight, Reader, I wonder was she using this to create a sense of urgency for my absentee father's involvement? Or, was this some deranged form of acceptance and/or a sadistic experiment?

Because of her, I was introduced to Correctol (laxatives created for women) and Fleet enemas around the same age.

Voice and Valor

"Abuse is abandonment because when children are abused, no one is there for them" (John Bradshaw)

Voice and Valor

I had genuinely wished I had Diana Prince's powers while I lived off and on in the small two-bedroom project apartment between the ages of two and six. Mother Free-Spirit and her ex-husband, Jheri, were my guardians at that time. He was physically abusive to her, and I often felt powerless and afraid to defend her. Thankfully, he never laid a hand on me, even when I deserved a spanking. At thirty-six, I learned from my biological father (Regular Lee Alone) why Jheri always left the corporal punishment to Free-Spirit; after the two men fought, Regular told him that although Jheri couldn't be stopped from hitting Free Spirit, he was never to touch me!

One day, however, I heard Jheri ask Mother Free-Spirit why I was making "that sound." I was in my room pretending one of my stuffed animals was giving birth to a crying baby.

It was a warm Friday night when the dysfunctional adult pair were seated amicably in the living room.

I was six years old and in my bedroom when I overheard Free-Spirit mumble to Jheri.

"Watch this." She elevated her voice and called me, "Dante, come to Mother please!"

Voice and Valor

I remember it feeling a bit strange, but I cheerfully emerged in their presence.

"Yes?"

Always a stickler for basic skills, Free-Spirit called out, "Dante, what is one hundred plus one hundred?"

"Two hundred!" I declared brightly and ran back in my room.

They both cheered. She clapped her hands in celebration and thought of a new problem for me.

"Come back and tell me what is two hundred plus three hundred?"

I thought about it and ran to where they could see me and yelled, "Five hundred!"

I was beginning to enjoy the game Mother Free-Spirit, Jheri, and I were creating.

They cheered me on again.

Jheri appeared impressed. "Yaaay, he's smart, isn't he?"

"Mmm-hmm, Dante, what is eighty-nine plus fifteen?"

I crept back into their sight with a

bewildered expression. Although intelligent enough to add the two big numbers and bring down the zeros in the first two mental math problems, I was unaware of how to arrive at this latest sum.

"I don't know how to do that one."

A fan of mathematics as well, I continued to ponder, raising my head in the air trying to solve it. Suddenly, Free-Spirit's tone turned cold and intimidating.

"You don't know how to do it? How could you so easily add numbers way bigger than those and can't add two smaller ones?"

I lowered my head to look at her expression and began to cower in fear. I took a stuttered breath while trying to overcome the tyranny of her logic. I added, "M-my teacher never taught us that yet."

She ominously rose from the sofa and closed in on me. I gulped as she walked up and spat, "You don't know it? What do you mean you don't know it?!"

Tears began welling up in my eyes as I looked up at her in terror while desperately combing my memory to see if I had failed to pay attention in class. For the life of me, I knew I hadn't yet been taught how to "carry the one." Suddenly, she grabbed me and snatched me into the bedroom. I'd had enough "sane" spankings to know what was coming next.

While writing this, I painfully remembered the jittery sound in my throat, my trembling lips, and the sheer panic I felt as she man-handled me. I pleaded "nooo!" and instantly regretted I'd said it as I looked into her terrible eyes.

We reached the edge of my bed.

"Take off your pants!"

"No, please, please. I don't know it. My teacher hasn't taught us that yeeet!"

She yelled her command again and told me I'd better be done when she got back. I knew she'd be heading out the front door to strip branches from the tree near our apartment.

Jheri came to the doorway, nonchalantly, as I removed my shoes and slowly lowered my pants. Cold air hit my legs as I imagined the pain I was about to feel. My eyes pleaded with him to rescue me, but he only put his hands into his pockets.

"We were going to surprise you and take you to McDonald's if you had said the answer."

I looked at him through tears, whimpering

and confused, wondering why I was being punished for a reward I didn't ask for or could even earn at that point. Unfair and emotionally abusive, they knew I considered going to McDonald's a treat.

Suddenly, I heard Free-Spirit return and the sound of her tearing leaves from the thick limbs she'd torn down. I curled myself up on the bed as I uttered the most heart-wrenching "Ahhh, Mother, nooo! Stooop, I don't know iiit!"

She began wailing on me repeatedly. I squirmed, kicked, and screamed, trying desperately to shield my legs from the stings. Free-Spirit paused momentarily, never breaking eye-contact from my welting legs.

"Move your hands!" Although I hesitated and cried, she insisted. "Move your hands, Dante." The moment I complied, she resumed swinging the branches against my young shins and thighs.

Mother Free-Spirit stopped after a few horrifying minutes. I continued to cry.

"I'm going to get you some paper and a pencil, and you will stop pretending you don't know how to do this problem."

"But, I don't!" She faked a swing of the branches at me. I flinched and moaned, instinctively holding out my protective hands and recoiling my stinging legs. I was tired, trapped, and petrified.

Free-Spirit stormed out of my room and reappeared with the promised articles. Angrily, she bore down on my dresser under one of my Dr. Seuss books writing down the problem I didn't solve.

As she wrote, the tyrant issued a damning imperative.

"If you keep acting like you don't know how to do this problem, then I will return again and again, adding more and more switches each time."

She passed me the "shotgun" homework and stormed out toward the front door.

Under absolute duress, my hands and legs stung as I tried to solve the problem. I remember Jheri never left my doorway and I being afraid but bravely whispering to him, asking if he could help. While recalling these events decades later, I realize Jheri must have deliberately withheld his knowledge of how to solve this basic math problem. It wasn't until after Mother Free-Spirit's second attack on me that he lied down beside me yelling.

"Boy, you better do that problem before Mother Free-Spirit comes back in here with more switches!" Thinking back, I knew he resented the fact that I wasn't a "real boy."

I could tell she was standing in the living room growing in fury, feeding on Jheri's affirmation of her sadism, and savoring my fear. The sound of leaves snapping from the unseen mound of switches rang in my ears. If Free-Spirit had been identified and medicated by then, I wouldn't be writing this.

Through slobber, pain, confusion, frustration, and terror, I begged him, "I don't know how to do it! Can't you teach me? Pleeease!"

As if on cue, Jheri rolled his eyes, sighed, and backed off the bed as his wife rushed in and resumed smashing branches upon my leaking legs. By this time, my lower limbs were nearly numb, but I lied there wishing for my grandma, grandad, or maybe even death. I had no idea when this cycle of torture — her voice, his voice, and mine — was going to end.

The fourth or fifth whipping terminated her vehemence. She snatched the homework, pencil, and book from my bed. I remember the wrinkled, yellow legal pad paper had small streaks of my blood, sweat, tears, and her leaves on it. She sentenced me to bed as an expressionless Jheri

71

walked away. Ever so carefully, I climbed under my sheets and comforter. Fragments of a tree slid down my blanket as I gingerly accommodated myself. I trembled and winced as the fabric touched my open wounds. The fetal position was not ideal under these circumstances, but it comforted me. She flicked off the light, gave me an irritated "goodnight," and closed the door. I smothered my emotions, and I repeated the salutation out of obligation, knowing if I hadn't, I'd receive more pain. Still, I wailed a little as I said it. I cried a cry that begged for her comfort and explanation. She huffed at my dismay, making me feel like a sissy. I don't remember if I had dinner that night.

The lingering scent of switches, Free-Spirit's adrenaline, my fear, and a twisted energy danced in my nostrils as my head settled onto my cold pillow. It was dark when I felt moonlight on my face. I listened to their muted voices as they left the house, perhaps going to McDonald's without me. A tear slid down my nose.

Exhausted and relieved it was over, I asked myself, *What had I done? Had I not paid attention in school? I could have sworn I hadn't learned how to add like this yet. Was I busy chattering while this was being taught? If so, why couldn't I have remembered and saved myself from those beatings?*

Voice and Valor

What had I done to deserve this? Should I tell Grandma? Or anyone? Will Free-Spirit challenge me again? Why didn't she hear me when I told her I honestly didn't know how to solve eighty-nine plus fifteen? Why did Jheri ignore me and refuse to rescue or at least help me? If I told Grandma and Grandad, would they have believed me? And, if they did, would Mother Free-Spirit make up a lie, justify and minimize her brutality, and punish me at the first opportunity for telling on her? Something deep inside me said I was on my own. I don't know when I finally drifted off to sleep.

Fast forward; I had kept all this to myself until I was in my early thirties, recalling the abuse as if it had just happened while undergoing deliverance counseling. I tapped into the broken child inside me. The bull-like spirit of pride manifested, telling me and the deliverance team that they had no right to expel him because he, not God, had protected me from Mother Free-Spirit! I even blamed God and myself for allowing that to happen to me. Why hadn't I been stronger? False guilt, as I now know.

In hindsight, I remember while still at age six discounting my suspicions that Free-Spirit had set me up. She had been a teacher's aide in the past before I started elementary school and was most

73

likely very well aware of the pacing guide. Free-Spirit also knew I liked mathematics a lot and was confident about my abilities. She betrayed me and used these qualities against me. Why was she belittling me?

I can recall my inner voice saying, *Oh, okay, that is how you do this* when months later my teacher taught us when to carry a one when adding numbers whose sum reached or exceeded ten. Repressing again, I choked a sob back into my throat as I sat among my classmates.

I wondered much later as an adult if she was trying to beat away her shame of me. Did she blame herself for my "tendencies"? Or, was she trying to beat "that spirit" out of me? While editing this section of the book you're holding, I read a 2012 web article about a North Carolina pastor who told his congregation to beat the gay out of four-year-olds, to give the boy a good punch, and to break his limp wrist. I know I will most likely never be able to voice my feelings to Free-Spirit because of her having been diagnosed as manic bipolar and her human penchant for deflection, denial, and defensiveness. As with her older sister, Sweet, I had to learn to forgive and continually re-forgive them (and others) without the apology.

Voice and Valor

"Christians must confront their fears about homosexuality and curb the humor and discrimination that offend homosexual persons"
(Berzon and Leighton)

Voice and Valor

A friend once told me that one of the reasons he stopped going to church was because pastors usually ended up saying something stupid across the pulpit. His mother had asked him and his partner to attend a church service with her. Sure enough, the minister began ranting to a packed congregation, "I pray that when you eat McDonald's food, [that your] guts rot!" The pastor was angry that the immensely successful franchise had been a supporter of gay rights. My friend looked around, confident that someone would have an adverse reaction, yet no one said anything. The church was dead silent. My friend told me the only thing that kept him in his seat was his respect for his mother.

Sometime before I heard this story, I viewed a YouTube recording of a Christian conference tailored for men which was headed by a famous preacher, the late Dr. Myles Munroe, whom I greatly admire because of many of his other teachings. As an aside, I particularly chose not to disguise his name due to my sincere respect for his extraordinary legacy. However, the shrewd man seemed to have been losing his audience's attention and shifted into criticizing men for being physically attracted to other men. He used both hands to air sketch the "appealing" curvatures of the female form. Then, he turned his back to deliberately exemplify the "dull" straightness of the male backside. Many of the guys leapt to their feet clapping, cheering, and whistling in support of the minister's crude, derogatory humor against homosexual men. Was this necessary? Would this win gay men and/or women to Christ?

Many Christians speculate that Jesus's and God's reaction to homosexuality matches homophobic, hate-filled attitudes. Readers, I believe Jesus confronted every kind of human being we witness today. Imagine, if you will, how Jesus would have responded to a homosexual. The average contemporary conservative would have expected Him to shame and humiliate him/her. However, studies show that Jesus had, in fact, encountered a centurion soldier whose slave boy was sick unto death; the original text reveals that the soldier's young servant was his male lover. The officer wanted them to be able to make love to each other again and Jesus, aware of the culture (Greek: *pais*) and human sexual orientation, applauded the centurion's faith, made no mention of "sin," and restored the servant boy without bias. Christ's passion was to reconcile all mankind to His Father by demonstrating unconditional love, eternal truth, mutual respect, and human compassion.

This type of discrimination, however, is not

exclusive to male preachers. I remember being
asked to play the flute for an evening church
anniversary service. Having not picked up the
instrument in years before that performance, I felt a
bit dizzy and disoriented afterward due to the
atrophy of my lung power, the anointing generated,
and the demands of being re-acclimated to that type
of ministry. Other men and women, boys and girls,
contributed to the service as well. The brother who
led praise and worship was awesome, and his
singing literally brought in the manifested presence
of God. Also present was Second Husband, the
master of ceremony and son-in-law of Sweet. The
host pastor of the church, Prophet Joy, stood up for
closing remarks. She, a good friend of Apostle
Sweet, thanked everyone for supporting but sternly
commended the organist for not having any "sugar
in his tank."

Anthony Stanford wrote,

> *Indeed, Black clerics who fit the
> persona of someone willing to
> demonize LGBTs and were
> already in sync with the self-
> righteous white evangelical
> extremists could be counted on
> to use their religious influence
> to persuade their [audience] of
> the Black community to go*

Voice and Valor

*along with the strategy of social
exclusion and sexual bias
against LGBTs.*

When you're openly or suspected to be a
gay man, some people readily try to call/treat you
like you're a "girl." I imagine this translates
conversely for non-heterosexual females who are
told they are *trying* to be a "boy." No one should
presume anything on anyone. Truth told, neither
effeminate nor masculine mannerisms are clear
indicators of a person's sexual preference. Think
about it; Reader, have you or someone you know
been profiled based on their attire, behavior in a
moment, or residence? Assumptions and stereotypes
are always rude and hurtful. Jesus never mistreated
outcasts, and preachers misrepresent Him when
they do this.

Wisecracks and bold statements are some
things to which non-heterosexuals are all too
accustomed — but to behave this way in Jesus's
name? Anyone paying attention and from the Black
community knew she was exposing and putting
down the remaining men for "struggling" with
homosexuality. Joy's segment had suddenly
morphed into a small campaign against non-
heterosexuals. Honestly, I stood up and clapped
with most other congregants in an awkward attempt

to cover my identity while simultaneously feeling betrayed by her and angry at myself and my cowardice!

I was in my early thirties at this time but hadn't yet fully reconciled my sexuality and spirituality. I was, however, all too familiar with being labeled "suspect." It was never a pleasant feeling, usually unwarranted, and always mean-spirited. I once heard a person say that being outed is like being stripped naked in a cafeteria full of onlookers and being forced to eat alone.

Years before Prophet Joy pastored her own church, she, Sweet, and I attended the same church under Apostle Pimp. Joy was his third wife. Actively "forgetting those things which were behind me," I served faithfully, strongly desiring the Pentecostal deliverance flair that the founding leader promoted. I horribly underestimated the man's homophobia. He'd make off-color comments in conversation and, while preaching, say things such as "you all know about my war against the gays" and "those with *that* spirit have to be chained to the altar." His personality was Dominant and Influential. Apostle Pimp was brilliant, unattractive, charming, opportunistic, and an excellent preacher. He could hardly wait to take credit for "delivering" me from homosexuality.

Voice and Valor

One Saturday, while hanging out with the leader and the brothers of our church, we were making fun of effeminate men. Each of us took turns mimicking "sissies" and laughing at each other. Normally, I was too paranoid about my own mannerisms but risked exposure. The apostle proudly declared to me, "I'm going to pay you the greatest compliment anyone has ever paid me. You would make a horrible faggot."

Ironically, the Apostle used to be a pimp and was guilty of having performed gay favors in the past. I had returned to support Sweet one Sunday morning, after I had withdrawn my membership from his church. I sang the sermonic selection. The service was over when Apostle Pimp asked me why I had not told him face-to-face that I was leaving. He had found the sealed letter in his mailbox.

Unflinchingly, I grinned, looking him in the eye, and said, "I wasn't in the mood to be manipulated."

"And, you think I'd do that to you?"

Becoming annoyed, I smirked. "Of course, you would have."

"I need you."

"What? What do you mean you need me?"

Voice and Valor

He stepped in close to my ear.

"I *need* you." His voice took on a harsh, breathy whisper as if attempting to seduce me.

I was in disbelief! This man thought that approaching me in this manner would have lured me back under his leadership. Even though I was "wrestling" with my sexuality, I still had standards. He wasn't at all a temptation for me. I never would have even masturbated about Apostle Pimp. This man considered me perverse, but he was the real pervert.

A common fallacy/ignorance is that gay men are attracted to all men and that bisexual people want every man and woman they see. That would be quite exhausting! After all, non-homosexuals aren't sexually attracted to every one of the opposite sex, if so, then there exists a strong problem with lust and potential sexual addiction. I'll never forget the intelligent African-American male pastor who spoke up for homosexuals in his huge congregation saying, "Leave gay people alone. They aren't bothering you. In fact, some of you are avoiding sitting next to them when they aren't even thinking about you. They need the same God you do, and that's why we're all here."

Grasping the reality of this conversation

Voice and Valor

with Apostle Pimp, I cast a disgusted look and viewed him up and down. He needed to be exposed! People were all around engaged in conversations of their own. I came ever so close to loudly expressing my acute discomfort at his sexual advance but merely backed away. At the time, I had no idea if anyone would have believed me. Those who preoccupy themselves with the topic of homosexuality are most often guilty of having engaged in its behaviors.

I never returned to that church and did not voice this encounter to anyone until many years later. I found that for many other reasons, Apostle Pimp's church folded.

Voice and Valor

"When you listen carefully to the stories of many gay [Christians] in both official and unofficial Church ministries, you hear expressed deep feelings of new faith, a sense of hope in themselves and others, and an experience of love in their choices about their sexuality" (Berzon and Leighton)

Rehearse the above quote contemplatively;
en you listen… carefully… to the stories… of
… gay Christians…" Everyone has a voice,
people want to listen or "hear"? Seemingly
pecially if you're suspected or believed to be
terosexual. Everyone has a story — one that
long before we met them.To be absolutely
nd certain, I never chose my attractions to
xes just as I never chose God's calling me to
-fold ministry. I, like any other yielded
fell in love with God, and He showed me
d mighty things! Heterosexuals are neither
ed or anointed by God than their
arts, despite common church ideology.

Also, "gay Christian" sounded oxymoronic,
even to me at first, at second, at third… until I gave
myself permission to think. I had to stop looking
outside of myself. Despite having great examples of
positive, super-confident gay, same God-believing
homosexual people in my contact list, I decided to
validate my inner truths. I had long accepted my
Christian identity since childhood. I had equally
suppressed my homosexual attractions in attempts
to please God.

Reader, do you also find it weird that those
who don't know what it's like to be gay have so
much to say to those who live it every day? No one

85

knows what it's like to self-confront the choice between oneself and one's faith unless they are a *different* Christian. This is largely due to the power of traditional biblical teachings, religious biases, and the fact that homosexual Christians are labeled hypocrites, therefore deserving second-class treatment and/or exclusion. Galatians 3:28, AMP states, *There is [now no distinction in regard to salvation] neither Jew nor Greek, there is neither slave nor free, there is neither male nor female; for you [who believe] are all one in Christ Jesus [no one can claim a spiritual superiority].* Even if I had backslidden from the Lord, which I have/would not, all followers of Christ are commanded to be spiritual and to practice a restorative, unconditional love. Gays are too often the condition, despite God's unconditional grace bestowed on mankind, humankind.

In May of 2018, I edited this autobiographical section about two weeks after an odd conversation with Color, a Christian, outside-the-box-thinking friend, and former pastor. We are in complete agreement with the realities of spiritual abuse, church hurt, religiosity, and the need for "an awakening," In reference to gays, Color was well-meaning and said, "*They* just need love and the word. That's all." Despite her best intentions and efforts to fear (respect) the Lord, her assertion still registers as a religious belief that gays need a *special* dose of God's love and God's word that is divinely set aside for non-heterosexuals. She and others who think along these lines reinforce a subtly prejudice "us vs. them" mindset that is demeaning. It reminds me of an ex-racist who is steadily deprogramming from racist ideologies.

Reader, although you've read some of my stories, there are two who have heard about my past drama with females before you. Fierce, Color's closest female friend, roommate, and right hand got up the courage one day to ask me if my historical problems with women was the only reason I didn't want to remarry. I told her I knew she'd suspected I was gay; Color had already told me months before that Fierce *saw* that in me. I told Color I was bisexual, but people accept gay better — go figure! The ladies and I routinely had deep, transparent discussions about life, ministered prophetically to one another, and they appreciated the much needed enlightenment I gave them on the male psyche. The two were seeking relationships with males. Good men were, apparently, hard to find. Also, I was already well into the process of fully accepting myself and needed to practice coming out because I had a book to write. Color, who is very prophetic and a philosopher in her own right, listened intensely and seemed to understand my perspective.

Fierce, shrewd and protective, paid attention as well, but I, unknown to Fierce, observed that her reservations were more apparent than Color's. They seemed to have "understood" that day and treated me still with love and respect. We commented on how freeing the conversation must have been for me. I left their house with mutual laughs, sincere hugs, etc., yet by the following Sunday, I noticed a turn in both females. I imagined co-dependence and the homophobic loyalty to certain scriptures fueled their shift. One of them said twice during our gathering that "some people think that because their [spiritual] gifts still work that they are *okay* with God." I was betrayed and scapegoated again…, but this time in Jesus's name. While I fully understand that one must vote their conscience with regard to the Word of God as it is well-intentioned, to delegitimize anyone's personal relationship with Jesus and then passive-aggressively put-off on the very one who bared his/her soul to you isn't godly at all. Jesus protected the dignity of those he served.

Conviction is not the word to describe what happened. This was homophobia, bias, and religious behavior. Too often our "Christian duty" conflicts with our sense of trust.

Voice and Valor

Those who find themselves disgusted at the numbers of homosexual people in the world tend to respond with a tribal, militant attitude. With an acutely self-righteous tone they said, *"That spirit* is running rampant, even in clergy!" Toxic shame, more accurately, is more *rampant* than homosexuality itself. According to N. Cindy Trimm, in her *The Rules of Engagement,* our societies, churches, and homes can be shame-based.

As you read in the first vignette, when homosexual behavior is involved, it doesn't matter how many positive qualities you possess. God can anoint you, but hetero-bias people will use their issue with your personal issues against you, show you a glass ceiling, and belittle your greatness. Again, no one knows the struggle of reconciling one's own sexuality with one's own faith. Becoming valorous is always first mental. Thank God!

Religious people are full of tradition and contradictions, which have nothing to do with how God feels. Too many believers assume it is their duty, because of their own hang-ups, to determine not only the authenticity of a gay Christian's profession of his/her relationship with God but also his/her eternal destination after death. Hetero-bias individuals too often stop *listening… carefully.*

Voice and Valor

Jehovah God is omnipotent, omnipresent, sovereign, and inescapable. And, although He lives inside the hearts of welcoming Christians, God's individuality and opinions remain separate from His hosts. His children forget this often. Still, the Lord is immensely personal. King David understood that God is ever-mindful of everyone, sharing with us that we were all "fearfully and wonderfully made" and "curiously wrought in secret." The biblical prophet, Jeremiah, knew all too well that the Creator knows more about us at conception than we do. He, however, wants to tell us if we can allow ourselves to *listen carefully* to deep feelings of *new faith, hope in themselves and others,* and *experience of love.*

Mark 7:12-14, the TLB version, speaks of traditions we hold in our heart as follows: *And so you break the law of God in order to protect your man-made tradition. And this is only one example. There are many, many others. Then Jesus called to the crowd to come and hear. All of you listen... and try to understand.*

Readers, if we are truly listening, then we will experience true valor, inner struggle with religiosity/traditionalism in our own hearts. The voice of Holy Spirit wants to tell us that we, ourselves, have more problems with other people's lives than He does.

Moreover, my initial worship experiences in the 1980s were among Disciples of Christ with my grandparents, mother, and a majority of my uncles and aunts. They were active in the church, and most of my family could sing well. All of us sang in at least one of the choirs. We also attended vacation bible school each summer. As a youth, I liked church, music, and Holy Spirit praise breaks. A majority of Black church worship experiences in this era commonly involved what we called "shouting," not with the voice, particularly, but with spontaneous dancing or physical responses to His touch. The organist and drummer assisted the praisers resulting in an uproariously glorious manifestation of God's presence. I was afraid to "shout," in accordance with my youthful experience and persistent fear of coming off as effeminate.

Furthermore, the Painters, essentially Grandma, Sweet, Spicy, Jew, and Muscle got involved with a noon-day prayer group, which later became an unofficial bible school. This association afforded my family with our first experiences with witchcraft and spiritual abuse. Grandad, for that very reason, discerned this before we did and stopped going even if he could not prevent his wife and children from it. Nevertheless, it was at one of those meetings that I received Jesus into my heart, was baptized in Holy Spirit, spoke in tongues, and even witnessed an exorcism during the summer.

At home we listened to classic, African-American 1980s Gospel artists, with my hometown having birthed a long list of extraordinarily talented church and community choirs as well. Although there was an appreciation for 1960s and 70s R&B, our family concept of godliness was shifting our musical diet. I routinely pretended to direct the imaginary choir while listening to records on our turntable stereo in the living room. I had a high voice and enjoyed singing the soprano lines and a famous alto with the sweetest voice soon caught my attention. I remember singing to *Up Where We All Belong*, for example, which resonated within me for duplicitous reasons: I identified with females mostly, and my voice hadn't yet changed to support singing a full-grown man's lower range. I had already felt unfit to "try" to be a man, so singing like one made me feel even more awkward. Uncle Jew would honor me with his vocal presence rarely and sing the brother's lines. His mother and older sisters thought we sounded great and should enter talent shows, but Jew didn't want to be seen singing with a boy who sounded like a girl. This had only added more confusion since I was trying to project a mature tenor voice in our church's youth choir, but my prepubescent vocal chords hadn't yet developed to produce a manly sound.

Homophobic people, however, take every opportunity to turn/twist anything into a weakness, even a young boy's naturally high voice. I never told Uncle Jew, but I learned to pretend his and others' attitude didn't affect me. It used to be difficult to think he was also partially threatened by my potential. Be that as it may, little boys should never be shamed for not being "manly." I cringe inside when parents castigate their male children for not having bass in their voices.

As it was, I played football only a couple times with guys in the neighborhood; they knew I normally played with the girls. I could run fast, "juke," and leap over tacklers. Maybe they were going easy on me at first to build my confidence. Truth is, I was afraid of being hit and did whatever it took to avoid pain. Who didn't? My uncles made fun of me for being afraid of being hit. What they treated as abnormal was, indeed, normal. They once told me I should play basketball because I was, in their opinion, going to be too tall for football. Did you raise your eyebrow too? Also, the hyper-masculinity surrounding athleticism didn't appeal to my cerebral wiring. Were sports and women the only things which validated manhood? My uncles were my initial male role models.

By the time I entered middle school, Sweet and Spicy befriended some people from a White, charismatic, non-denominational church. Since it was Grandma's wish that we all continued going to church each Sunday, we received the words of life there. Our pastor was an eccentric, yet highly revelatory preacher/teacher who pastored a multi-cultural congregation. He subjected us to healthy ministry and supernatural encounters with Holy Spirit. I learned to appreciate praise & worship and moved away from Black choir-style music, as a result. Here, we gained a lifelong respect for the amazing Caucasian contemporary Christian music singers of the 1980s. I underwent a culture shock too, not only with regard to these artists but also with the preachers. We spiritually fed on the ministries of 1980s A-list televangelists. Seeing these artists and teachers in person at our local church was also a rare treat. Exposure to such diversity molded my perceptions of God, emotionalism, and my relationship with Him. Thankfully, at present, I am no longer overly critical of any expression of worship as long as God's presence can be detected.

I graduated from high school in 1994 with

Voice and Valor

the intentions of running away from God. As the Lord would have it, I joined my university's Black student gospel choir, and received another culture shock. This was my first real experience with choir tenor; to me, it felt like I was being forced to sing alto! Although I had been taught and "homophobed" into believing that "real men" sang low, here I was eighteen-years-old, heavier voiced for a young man my age, and witnessing other men enjoying belting notes way beyond my emotional and vocal comfort levels. I had to "legalize" their pleasure and prowess in my head as I was introduced to the massive gospel music, *God is in Control*. Around this era, the production of gospel songs that challenged the upper ranges of average choirs was the musical fad. Choir masters from New York, Chicago, North Carolina, and the tri-city area of the Carolinas cemented their singers' mastery as they wrote music which modulated higher numerous times (above the average choir's abilities, or daring) or possessed crucial inversions. — For those of us who are unaware of what a musical inversion is, an instance would be when tenors suddenly sing the altos' line; the altos shift to the soprano part; and the sopranos take on the tenor part and begin singing the lower voice part eight pitches higher. — You can only imagine how these ultra-talented groups wowed their fans in person with at least two more modulations above that which they recorded.

I was not about to be outdone! Stretching my voice, I felt my personal status and esteem elevating as I practiced singing Black gospel music. Unfortunately, the males capable of achieving this feat were highly favored in our student group while second tenors, basses, and baritones experienced near-second-class treatment. By the time competition season arrived, I had managed to increase my range substantially and add power to my cords. Persistence and a little help from one of the guys with whom I was sexually involved earned me a spot in the tenor section for competition.

The next year, I remember losing my appetite for Black gospel music at that time because I began to truly hunger and thirst for something more. I had been exposed to Fred Hammond's new choir called Radical for Christ (RFC) and quickly identified with the Architect of Urban Gospel music's hybrid choir/praise team format. Millennial Christians would probably hardly imagine a time when praise and worship-style music wasn't the norm. During this time, praise and worship was still thought of as White music, where Blacks would have normally turned up their nose. Choirs and soul-stirring soloists ruled the Black church experience.

God used all of my singing in the college choir to stir my hunger for Him. I told you earlier how I was running *from* God. Instead, I ran right *to* Him.

I was then studying flute performance and became a music education major in college. I was literally burning out with all of the intense classical musical instruction I was receiving at university having been engulfed in it all throughout high school. So, I began to enjoy belting high notes among my collegiate peers, but God was calling me into an intimate relationship. My appetite for revelatory knowledge of God's word and a strong passion for praise and worship developed, as a result.

Interest in school and people-pleasing declining, I gathered my bible, journal, CD Walkman, and RFC's *Praise in the House* album. I stole away daily into my apartment complex's clubhouse to spend hours with the Lord. Before I knew I was transforming, God reaffirmed His love and acceptance of me completely. I had previously given my life to Jesus, but this time it wasn't in efforts to please others but for myself. These encounters were sweet, unforced, and free from religion as Holy Spirit taught me so much about God's voice and Himself, produced His fruit within me, and manifested my spiritual gifts. He taught me how to believe in Him and His workings without feeling it. I learned to truly take God at His word, that He had started His process and was actively completing it. I engaged in the spontaneous song of the Lord, without knowing what I was doing. I was free in Christ, needing no approval from preachers. All I wanted was God! He anointed me with a measure of His power and influence.

A week ago (May 2018), I began listening to Eddie James. His leadership and passion for God re-acquainted me with *me.* When Mr. James said that we must be fascinated with God, that reconnected me with my early RFC days, where I fell in love with God, private worship, revelation and adoration, intercession, and priestly authority. I am, finally, able to self-accept each aspect of my God-given individuality — intellect, sexuality, spirituality, personality, etc. — with a growing fluidity. I pray, Reader, you're finding this inspiring.

I know now that He was birthing the fathering spirit within me in the mid-90s. Unfortunately, pre-familiar internal conflicts with rejection and personal experiences with spiritual abuse, inevitably, altered my spiritual awareness.

Voice and Valor

"Underplaying the differences blinds us to the signature traits of other forms of social hatred. Indeed, in judging other prejudices by the one you know best, you may fail to recognize those other prejudices as prejudices" (Delroy Constantine-Simms)

Voice and Valor

"I'm telling you, Tamara, dealing with her nasty attitude makes it really hard to sing with her. She talked down to me like I was some little child, and it was only because we were in church that I didn't say more than I did. Just because she is much older than me, I'm not about to let her speak to me that way again,...something's got to be done about her."

Walking toward our cars after an evening rehearsal, I had begun venting my frustrations about a fellow tenor. Tamara was our worship leader; she was anointed, efficient, influential, and a very talented singer.

"Shhh, she's right there behind us," Tamara mumbled.

I glanced over my shoulder and saw Bridgette, the female tenor I was discussing. Even though I hardly cared whether or not she heard me, I conceded. I waited until Tamara and I were out of the accused one's earshot.

Our cars were parked diagonally from each other. Being a gentleman and wanting to reach out to a leader, I implored Tamara, "I had this similar problem with Bridgette before you came back. She and I were pulled into counseling before you returned, but her attitude was never properly dealt with."

Tamara said, "Mmhmm, I've seen *the spirits.*"

Immediately taken aback by her ominous pluralization of "spirit," I was instantly polarized by her double-talk. Duplicity is a symptom of religiosity.

If homosexuality was a spirit, then why is it that so many people aren't heterosexual? Jesus never addressed/fixated on this human trait. The Godhead is always inclusive, but too many Christians are exclusive.

Still, holding on to hope, I didn't want to believe I was being pushed back into the shadows…again. Here I was 39 years old and feeling like I did as a child.

"What do you mean by that?"

"Nothing, I'm just letting you know I see the spirits." She got in her car, breaking eye contact. It is amazing that people like Tamara feel as though they're doing something original. Single, lonely, opportunistic, and prejudiced, she unwittingly identified herself to me.

I smirked and said, "Mmhmm, sure you

are." I could tell she disliked my response.

I had briefly watched Tamara get into her car before climbing into my own. Trying desperately not to over-react to her passive-aggressive bait and switch, her word choice revived familiar uncomfortable feelings. I and so many others despise the injustice of being "outed." What did her suspicions about my sexuality have to do with my legitimate reservations about Bridgette? Absolutely nothing.

People find it difficult to think outside of a stigma (a mark of disgrace associated with a particular circumstance, quality, or person). Duplicity (deceit, double-dealing, and double-talk) is a common tool in personal interactions.

Most homophobic individuals, including immature Christians like Tamara, believe that my conflict with the notoriously difficult female tenor was due to my sexuality. In essence, their detestation with my "lifestyle" (another demeaning word) is the sole reason for all bad events in a non-heterosexual person's life. Conversely, they would not appreciate my saying, "So, the *good* things that happen to you are because you're *not* gay?"

White hegemony (WH) is a westernized ideology that states if you are not a White, heterosexual, wealthy, Christian man then you are defective. Therefore, non-Whites, LGBT+, members of middle and lower socio-economic classes, non-Christians, and women struggle the hardest in American society. White supremacists treated Blacks similarly as if to say *because you're a nigger you are entitled to second-class treatment and contempt.* Substitute any marginalized group — women, gays, less than wealthy, or what have you — and one can see the exclusions. Sociologists define prejudice as a negative outlook toward a person or group, based on the perceived characteristics of that person or group. Strikingly, prejudices (or biases) are often held independently of facts about the target(s). It's like the ever-lasting grudge.

Spiritual abuse, furthermore, is easy to deny because it is often very subtle. As previously stated, I too was raised Christian, but I had to deprogram myself from demonizing almost everything, especially homosexuals. Biases hide just as easily in church circles due to the traditional interpretations of Holy Bible. Acquiring slaves, mixing seeds or fabrics, eating shellfish, and being handicapped are examples of abominations in Levitical passages; however, King Solomon declared that a proud look, shedding innocent blood, and dividing people are also listed as things "God" hates. Still, too many Christians, ignore these references, readily preferring the sanctity of society. Verses addressing homosexuality remain over-emphasized and grossly misunderstood. Inconsistencies like these create a dichotomy between biblical interpretations and human realities. No intelligent person "chooses" an attraction that would invite people to be mad at you and verbally and/or physically abuse you.

Subsequent to Pastor Wise-Guy's ignorant assertion, Tamara became increasingly overt. Song lists were sent in advance, and a song I suggested and was slated to lead was mysteriously removed from the worship team emails. When I inquired of her, Tamara told me not to worry about it, leading me to believe it was out of her control. Furthermore, I was much taller than her, so she had to look up at me to frown when I missed a note or word to a verse while our team ministered during altar call. It was slightly embarrassing to me when a member of the congregation told me she witnessed Tamara's rudeness. Later, she began calling me "sensitive" in private and in front of others when I spoke up for myself (a trick many of my family members played on me growing up). Tamara must have thought herself to be testing my manhood, which is a common mistake single women make when screening for a mate. Men don't see this as a game but as emasculating and as a challenge. It is most often off-putting. She presumed she would be "booed up" by the following Valentine's Day (2016), but the bullying female remains single as of this writing.

It was humiliating to know you were being outed in secret conversations. One of Dr. Cindy Trimm's spiritual warfare books taught me that among many of the characteristics of gossip are speculation and pride. The target is often excluded from the side conversations and consensus. I was never dignified with a conversation, still, I waited too long to see if she and her cohorts would abandon their cowardice and simply talk *to* me — something that usually never happens. I also perceived that since the worship leader was gossiping, Tamara felt empowered to presume herself in my personal business. Her chiding was as if she was trying to force tears, a sob story, or a confession of my sexual identity.

I imagined her conversing with the pastor (and other members) about how I used my cell phone. The worship team sat on the front row of our growing mega-church, and mobiles were vital to intercommunication about song changes and feedback during services. Tamara would use her cell to text alerts, whomever else, and take sermon notes. I, like others, would message the team. Because it was unfitting to doze off during the pastor's messages, I often fought off sleep by playing games and/or responding to texts. At times, some communication, admittedly inappropriate, was with men on gay dating apps. I checked those messages like I would Yahoo emails, more motivated by boredom and habit but never for securing dates or visual pleasures. Non-sexual connections and great conversations can be formed on dating sites, too, since, I'm writing a tell-all.

I usually sat next to Tamara, and I believe she saw what I was doing. Instead of talking to me about it, the leader shared her concerns with the pastor, got his disapproval, and, clad with his negative opinion, used it as fuel to harass me. Treatment like this contributes to the feeling that you don't belong. Contemplations of my predicament reminded me of a hate sign I saw on a documentary; a racist's handwriting shouting, *Niggers, go home!*

Taking advantage of the fact that I would not make a scene, Tamara bullied me, putting me on the spot and talking to me as if I were less than a man. I remember when we had a guest worship leader rehearse with us. She knew the equally

106

homophobic man well. We singers had to quickly learn an incredibly wordy song, and I'd had a challenging week and was, therefore, unable to concentrate on the lyrics adequately. When the singers and I were asked if we had questions about anything before ministering, I asked for help with some words. Tamara, in front of the mischievous guest, his entourage, and my fellow songsters began badgering me. Her tone and posture signified her indignation at my queerness.

To the amusement of onlookers, she rehearsed the line, rolled and then stiffened her neck, "What else?"

When I looked at her with an awkward chuckle, I declined. She insisted. I got smart with her in self-defense, even though I minded my body language so as not to come off effeminate. Internally, I know that this weakened my conviction. But Tamara! She thought herself God of the situation, felt she had the upper-hand, and countered every attempt. My leader was determined to show me up in front of everyone. I strongly believed that if I had got in her face and intimidated her, people would have immediately jumped to her aid. Tamara gambled on this. Also, I was confident she wouldn't have admitted she was mistreating me, true to the behavior of bullies. My past experiences involve being scapegoated as a trouble-maker, and I wasn't ready to go through that again. Reminded me of what *they* called Blacks who spoke out against discrimination. I'm glad that I'm now more confident to stand up for myself, even in the faces of bible-wielding Christians.

The minister of music once told me, however, that Tamara thought of me as a punk but to let God handle her. I hated myself for grinning and bearing the torture. I soon confronted her on her bullying behavior, yet she denied it. On the worship team, I began to feel as though I had a voice but no voice.

Many professionals are coming/want to come out of the closet, but those who are ignorant to that journey can be very insensitive. I will not dare to compare one form of marginalization to another. Take a moment, however, and imagine the crap non-heterosexuals have to put up with on a regular basis; some heterosexuals disrespect or insult gays to make themselves feel better about their own sexuality.

Hetero-superiority is fragile yet prevalent. Parallel: Too many White people, for example, don't know what it's like to be Black in America. I heard a heckling young man say, "If I were gay, I'd kill myself." I witnessed one of my younger male cousins who was freshly released from prison say, "If I found out someone in our family was gay, I'd disown him from the family." White supremacists feel Blacks should be denied humanity just as homophobic individuals of all races feel non-heterosexuals should be controlled, institutionalized, and/or exterminated.

Thankfully, Jesus told John and James they had the wrong *spirit* (or attitude) and that He didn't come to Earth to destroy people but to save them. God gave humankind dominion over the world, but He never intended us to dominate each other. A full life was God's gift to everyone on Earth. Why don't all of our Christian brothers and sisters know and emphasize this? Why is it far easier to fear and remain ignorant?

Moving forward, my discomfort with revealing my sexuality was more out of a lack of support from my audience than it was with my resolve. The emotional abuse I was experiencing from Tamara was symptomatic of society and most Christians. Placed in this incredibly unfair predicament, I felt like the weakling she identified. I began feeling the anxieties akin to bullied children. *Should I leave? Should I stay? What do I say to get her to shut up? Who will I have to fight?*

Voice and Valor

Considering the enormous stigma on non-heterosexuality and imminent exclusion from the team, I didn't want to be dishonest, but it wasn't her place to expose me either. Many Christians feel it their duty to uncover people, especially those believed to have the "homosexual spirit." Jesus never did this, yet Tamara and I attended a church where the pastor admitted to confronting men passed thirty for being single. A prejudiced Pastor Wise-Guy would cop out on the issue of homosexuality saying he had no opinion on it. "God does though," and that's where he stood. He once admitted possessing a past hatred for gays but no present vehemence after he became a Christian.

I wasn't naive and didn't believe the arrogant leader. We are three-part beings — spirit, soul, and body. Holy Bible teaches us that upon heartfelt confession of Jesus Christ as Lord and His resurrection from the dead, it is only then that the human spirit is made instantly perfect. Far more spiritually mature teachers than Wise-Guy had taught me that our souls (individual mind) — will, emotions, memories, intellect, etc.— require a progressively collaborative renovation where individuals work with Holy Spirit, the Revealer of Truth, to realign his/her mind with God's. This, of course, takes a lot of time as our temperaments and personalities can be strong. Life influences our mindsets, rendering our wills yielding in some areas and completely unyielding in others. God is eternally all-knowing and good. Man knows good and evil. Satan is eternally evil. Reader, do you see the struggle?

However, while teaching during a worship service, Wise-Guy boasted his theory that 50% of the male population would be gay within the next fifty years. Typical to male dominance, Tamara's being female and 40+ aroused far less, if any, suspicion about her sexuality.

Ironically, Tamara shared with me her enormous concerns with the pastor's constant "grieving" of Holy Ghost, for example. We and countless others have been frustrated when he shuts Him down, and I supplemented our conversations with knowledge that my spiritual background included the tangible apostolic, prophetic, and exuberance of Holy Spirit. She reacted with mixed acceptance due to her prejudiced suspicions about my personal life. Which is worse, the perceiving homosexuality as sin or a bias against it? Could justifying such exclusion in our hearts be part of the reason why Christians have yet to do "greater works" as He commanded? Like most hypocrites, Tamara would talk *about* me to others about "my problems" and *at* me because of them.

The next time I saw her, she had already ended her intenerate ministry with that church a second time. Tamara addressed me with a wary respect in front of others at a birthday celebration. I didn't ignore her rather witnessed her other "personality." Where there is hypocrisy (by biblical interpretation, word, or deed), there is fraud. No matter how accomplished, flawed, or positive a Black person is, to too many he will always be just a nigger. Likewise, no matter how anointed, competent, kind, or successful a non-heterosexual is, to stiff-necked, prejudiced ones, he will always be a faggot and she a dyke. Sexuality isn't prejudiced to age, sex, race, ethnicity, religion, or even familial guidance.

Voice and Valor

"Despite their 'in control' exterior, men often feel like impostors and are insecure that their inadequacies will be discovered" (Shaunti Feldhahn)

Voice and Valor

"Dad, can I say something?"

I glanced to the right toward my 12-year-old ex-stepson. Placing my hands deeper into my pockets, I smiled a bit and nuzzled my mouth into the collar of my coat. It was the snowiest winter Connecticut had in years.

"Sure, go ahead."

"Mom prayed and asked God for a man of God. God sent her one, but she still wants to be the head of the house." He was sharp and well-disciplined and knew his mother was being disrespectful.

Xavier ("X" for short) had asked to walk to the movie theater with me just after a heated discussion between Lady O and me. Another one that she started.

Not that I ever would have minded, but she insisted he go with me. Fear that I was going to visit another woman motivated her. I never understood why angry women picked fights with men, drove them away, and then readily accused of running to another woman's side. Mind you, Reader, I had just moved to her hometown in CT just before the previous Thanksgiving. Whom did I know? No one besides her parents and a married couple, both of whom liked me right away. Lady O, on the other hand, had the guilty conscience.

Even though I felt vindicated and embarrassed at X's question, his acumen reminded me of my own at his age. He knew I wasn't athletic but looked up to me as his hero. We bonded while tossing a football and playing video games.

"I don't know, Son. I don't know." I sighed in efforts to keep from venting to a youngster, trying not to disrespect his mother to him.

We enjoyed our movie and returned home. Alexandria, who was five, was glad to see her brother and step-father.

A couple of days later, Lady O started another argument, blaming me for not *understanding* the problem. We were in our bedroom, and our voices were slightly elevated. I was not yet aware that she was already cheating on me (within the first three months of our marriage).

She was out to emasculate me. Never in my life had I repeatedly felt such a strong lack of a sense of belonging. Impostor.

Our bed had no head- or foot-board, but we sat with pillows between our backs and the wall. Frustration had set in. I calmed myself.

Voice and Valor

"You know? The kids see how you treat me like you're the head of our family. Don't you think that it's important for them to see us getting along?"

Lady O lifted her face from her hands, feigning ignorance.

"What are you talking about?" Her irrational anger always drove me crazy, although I managed to maintain my composure. I disliked arguing, especially within earshot of others.

Instinctively, I knew she was faking. The precariousness of my position was that I was made to feel like I was being chauvinistic or insecure for simply wanting respect from my wife. I was fully aware that too many men have abused their rightful authority, and women are often afraid of being bossed that fearful females buck against the pettiest things. I was desperate.

"X asked me one day why did you pray for a man of God, and then God sends you just that, and you still want to be the head?"

She attempted to hide a stupor; the grin liars manifest when they're busted. "No, he didn't. You're making that up!"

"No, I'm not and wouldn't do that. How smart were you when you were his age?"

Voice and Valor

"Whatever. I'm going to ask him."

The lady got up and pulled on her pants. How was she angry one minute but now appearing like a woman running to mischief? To her, this was a game.

She left the room.

I sat there alone, bewildered, confused, drained, lost, not praying, praying, and trapped. Here I was trying to be the best man, man of God, husband, father, priest, and example I could be in a marriage which never even saw a honeymoon, literally or figuratively.

Racking my brain, I knew there was something incomplete about the notion of "happy wife, happy life." I wanted to be happy too. Was that wrong? Naturally, Lady O, my wife, was the only way I could know if I was getting marriage right.

By this time, Sweet had already betrayed my confidence about "my past," but I horribly underestimated the degree to which the cunning Lady O would use it against me. I'd had no same-sex encounter in over five years, "walking in my deliverance," and was genuinely married — in my heart and mind. I loved being a husband. I loved being a dad. Even though I hadn't yet been properly educated about sexuality, I wasn't "playing a role" or "on the down-low."I was committed and content with being married to this woman and her kids. It took me over a year after the divorce to stop referring to Xavier and Alexandria as "my kids." Additionally, her own mother, Mrs. Marian, adored me and I her. She even defended me against her own daughter many times because she knew Lady O's temperament.

Still, she made me feel like an impostor, as if I was doing something wrong. We hadn't been married a week before she had begun picking verbal and physical fights. Socialized to "take it," to "be a man," and not to give up when marriage gets tough, I tried my best to hang in there. I wasn't the "bad guy."

I had never been validated as a man growing up and was ashamed to ask if I was doing it correctly. However, I knew I was a good man. Men who later live apart from their wives (some straight, openly gay or closeted) are often assumed to be the reason their marriage dissolves. Why is a gay divorcee's sexuality automatically the culprit?

Lady O even went as far as to play the "opposite game" with a dream she had. Using my past against me, she told me she dreamt she was sleeping with another woman.

This lunatic also attempted to validate herself with Sweet.

"She is his wife. She can *see,* and she would know her husband!" Mind you, the overbearing, super-spiritual Sweet and I first met the beautiful, deceptive Lady O at the same church event. We were married three months later.

Our rocky union lasted about a year and a half. Lady O was remarried two months after divorcing me and was with him less than three years (if that). It was rumored that she rekindled a relationship with an ex-boyfriend who got married behind her back. Turns out, Lady O had rushed me into marrying her in spite of him. The woman he married died of cancer, and Lady O is Mrs. Lady O a third time.

When people ask me why I am divorced, I tell them I wasn't perfect, but I wasn't the problem.

Voice and Valor

"Men would rather feel unloved than inadequate and disrespected" (Shaunti Feldhahn)

Voice and Valor

If ever anyone wanted to understand the emotions of the male species, then do/say something that makes him/her feel disrespected, manipulated, or tested. Men know this about each other and long for women to know the same. Just as there is such a thing as unconditional love, which women deserve, men desperately need unconditional respect, according to Dr. Emerson Eggerichs. It's his life-blood. Too many men can't articulate it and/or feel guilty asking for it, and far too many women understand it on a grossly superficial level.

Sadly, men have suffered an under-scrutinized, prolonged form of dehumanization until we have been, for the most part, socialized against emotional intelligence. When we express too much emotion (to each other or at all), we are made to feel uncomfortable with the warmth or pain in our own hearts. I once read that one of the top fears of American men is that he could be gay. We ask ourselves, "Does *feeling* make me *soft* or gay?" Insecure heterosexuals feel uncomfortable being sociable with people believed to be gay, and this basic cordiality makes non-gays question their own sexuality. I remember when I and other men had to make sure we were heard saying things like "I'm all man here," "no homo," "no gay-stuff, bruh," and/or following it up with a compensating macho gesture, anything to avoid social rejection. While so many of us understand this, why do we set each other up to be disrespected, as if it's not going to come back to bite us sooner or later? Homophobia produces a lot of actors.

I once posted a picture of myself on Facebook leading praise and worship. A Christian female minister commented, "Looking like Donnie McClurkin's nephew." I highly respect the multi-award-winning gospel artist and pastor and understand that many of us are aware of his testimony. Still, why the public comparison? Was this her passive-aggressive attempt to let me (and the world) know she knew "my secret"? No one likes being called out, but when you're perceived as gay some shady individuals justify their urge, even to the point of hiding behind religion.

When people, not just heterosexuals, feel superior to you, then they believe they can disrespect you. Too many Christians even think it their duty to "tell [you] the truth in love" where the telling is opportunistic and forced; "truth" is harsh, and usage of the word "love" is a cover. If readers don't understand my meaning, please notice there is usually no prevailing compulsion with regards to obese people, for example. Because being overweight is not considered by society to be a "big one." Jesus Christ said that blaspheming His name would be forgivable; however, blaspheming Holy Spirit cannot be forgiven. The latter is Jesus's only "big one."

I remember asking a fellow Christian what "we" are doing.

Between services, Sicily sat herself between Tamara and me. Another male choir member, very effeminate but married to a woman, had already positioned himself behind me.

Sicily hadn't spoken to me all morning but was suddenly conversational. Weird. In a sudden and transparent ploy to appeal to my intellect, she said something to the effect of some radio scholar who theorized that the reason so many men are gay is because they were denied love from their biological fathers. The worship leader and the man behind me stopped conversing, listening to Sicily's "exposure."

This type of absurdity and over-simplicity is all too common among heterosexuals. Ironically, one of her sons is "suspect." And, although she's married to a man, Sicily is a bit hardcore herself.

I immediately responded, "So, a lesbian is

gay because her mother didn't love her too?"

She wore a deadpan expression as she stared at me, visibly shocked at my quick, apt, and powerful answer. While I didn't deny her disrespectful implication, I continued slightly louder. By the way, I already discerned she had been gossiping with the other two, sharing their suspicions about my sexuality. To show "disapproval" of another person's "lifestyle" often involves insulting them on some level… if you're asking the average Christian.

"Jesus reached out to the outcasts of His day. What are *we* doing? We are supposed to be working out our own salvation, minding our own business, and walking in love toward everyone," I declared. I could have cared less if she and her two conspirators "loved" me because I loved myself. But respect was due unconditionally, especially since I've never disrespected them.

Needless to say, the conversation was over. All she could do was sit quietly as I changed the subject altogether. I was fully experienced with the antics of busy-body women, judgmental Christians, and hyper-masculine men who presume it their duty to have "this conversation." Beyond disrespectful, these people feel as though gays have no rights to privacy.

With sincerest regard to my beautiful female counterparts, I've often wondered why so many of them feel like they can teach a man how to be a man. After all, this was the motivation for Sicily's confrontation. Men don't attempt to teach females how to be women. Moreover, I've witnessed bitter, unhealed single mothers claim Mother's Day and Father's Day vindictively exclaiming, "I'm the mother *and* the father!" While I understood their frustrations at having to compensate for the fatherly void, I always felt like they were disrespecting good men — single fathers, child mentors, grandfathers, male teachers, stepfathers, etc. Single dads don't celebrate Mother's Day.

Rodney (my great friend and a fellow author) and I have talked about everything under the sun, often pondering the female species. He spoke in general and poignantly one day saying, "Whenever it's *not* about them, women can't deal with it."

To most men, when their women behave this way, it communicates disrespect.

Voice and Valor

"Add sexual overtones to all the ways kids use relational bullying to systematically diminish a bullied child's sense of self-worth—sexual rumors or sexual epithets on bathroom walls or lockers, shunning a target because of his or her sexual orientation, 'scanning' a target's body, staring at breasts, leering, or making obscene gestures—and what you have is a hard-to-detect, easy-to-execute method of cutting to the core of the bullied kid" *(Barbara Coloroso)*

Voice and Valor

The quote above refers to minors. However, people of all ages bully, and I am but one living witness. In social situations, we send each other cues as to whether something is okay or not. As a current employee in the public school system, I try to alert my students to the power they have to prevent rebellious peers from continuing their disruptions. Simply choosing not to laugh at, side with, or minimize bad behavior sends a direct message to any wayward pupil. Although it is the teacher's authority to control their class, it is the students' responsibility to control themselves.

Some kids are genuinely unruly, and their parents believe the lies they tell them at home, especially when teachers are fed up with the prolonged lack of support from school disciplinarians and caregivers. Parents would do well to observe student conduct during classroom changes and choose to believe they use profanity, play on the cell phones, get out of their seats when the impulse hits them, do their hair or someone else's, criticize/talk back to teachers, openly decline to do classwork, and unashamedly attempt to converse about anything! — sex included — during instructional time... or any time, for that matter. Too many parents fail to teach their kids boundaries at home. This neglect manifests in school. Parents

Voice and Valor

who are their children's friends don't realize they are teaching their kids that all adults should treat them similarly. Our students seem not to understand authority. There is, indeed, a clash of values in academic settings: education (instructional technology and school environment) vs. entertainment (addiction to electronic devices and urban culture). Is it any wonder we have had to employ school security guards and city policemen? These realities are wide-spread in inner city school populations.

When I taught long-term, my kids did not get away with misbehaving. Yet, as adults, we tend to get on our kids for this wrong behavior while enforcing it between our own peer groups and community when it comes to taboo topics, namely non-heterosexuality.

Assumptions, assumptions. Everybody is naturally curious but too many settle for cruelty. Many, unfortunately, counted on my silence. Stunned and without the voice of a supportive father ringing in my conscience, I was often left to maneuver life's adversities and false accusations…unsuccessfully.

I remember when a popular, fellow adolescent boy suddenly whispered my name in class during an independent assignment. He suspected I wasn't "one of the boys" and quickly pointed at me. The crass youngster wrapped his hand around an invisible penis and moved his curled hand back and forth near his open mouth in sync with his tongue, poking the inside of his cheek. He winked at his admiring flunkies. All of this was planned and executed secretly for my humiliation. Although I knew I was different, was taught I wasn't supposed to like boys, and felt girls considered me a substandard choice, I had no interest or experiential knowledge of oral sex. My teacher was completely unaware of the torture I was enduring. I felt false guilt for something I hadn't even fathomed. Naturally, this encounter cut me to the core, and I knew I couldn't tell anyone about it for fear they'd say I deserved it.

Wikipedia's explanation of shame says that perpetrators believe that *you brought on yourself what we chose to do to you.* I later read where displacement, confusion, scapegoating, and a violation of boundaries are symptoms of shame-based systems in families, churches, and societies.

Ideas about sexual conduct were routinely placed in my head long before I willfully committed the acts. Sweet had already prematurely exposed me to the notion of a double life, and now these boys

Voice and Valor

assumed that I sucked penises. In hindsight, I view this boy's lewdness as a pseudo-invitation offered in a manner that simultaneously protected the pervert's macho reputation while subtly signaling his sexual interest in me to perform the act on him (or maybe vice versa). Reader, my situation may be a metaphor for your deepest, darkest private issue. You too know the injustice of being called out. The problem is with being non-heterosexual, it's sometimes difficult to determine a person's motives — be it malice, a cloaked flirtation, and/or displaced self-examination.

On the other hand, it was very common for boys to be curious about sex and be exposed to it, having stumbled upon pornography whether it belonged to their own father, an older sibling, or that of a friend's dad. I know of a couple boys who heard or walked in on their parents in various sexual positions. Sometimes, school boys shared secrets. I later learned that a few of us saw half-naked men emerging from their single moms' bedrooms, dangling penises swinging in the wind.

A preoccupation with penis size dominates male consciousness early in his development and can follow him into adulthood. Moreover, it even determined a boy's sexual prowess, self-esteem, and respect from the girls. As boys, we were peer-pressured to be sure as many people as possible knew we had a big dick. An inability to brag about "hurting a girl" constituted the boy had a small one. As an adult in my thirties, I recall a female asking whether or not my penis touched the water in the toilet when I sat. Confused, I answered yes (at times) but because I wasn't accustomed to making such a connection, I didn't readily know what that meant to her.

Boys, nevertheless, are peer-pressured with the rite of passage to be known for "humping" girls. They would testify to peeking into keyholes as they watched their older brothers have sex with girls they sneaked into the house while their parents worked. Oh, how I remember Cousin Q sharing his father's dubbed VHS pornographic video with me. Thankfully, we were always careful to rewind it to the spot where my uncle left it. Does this take anybody back?

Two years after Y2K, I joined a small church and played a beautiful hymn on the flute there. One of the deacons sexually harassed me. He made fun, asking me if I also played the "skin flute" to which I immediately snapped, "What is your problem?" He grinned. Very shortly thereafter, I reported this encounter to our pastor who was genuinely caught off guard at the content of my complaint. The exasperated leader's eyes widened as he looked down at his desk, leaning back in his swivel chair, leg crossed over his other thigh. I was confident that the dapper man would reprimand the offending deacon who was called into attendance as well. Pastor calmly asked the deacon to apologize for his antic to which the subordinate leader complied half-heartedly and I departed the session unsatisfied. It was as if the deacon had already rehearsed the joke secretly where both men probably laughed. After all, the senior leader didn't offer me an apology for his cohort's behavior. I also later found out that this deacon had a reputation for being rude and offending others within the assembly. Tiring of church, I soon relocated.

A distant future impromptu rap session with Apostle Pimp took place on a Saturday morning. The bully had already suspected I wrestled with "that gay spirit," especially since I played the flute, wasn't macho though masculine, and whatever else the preacher deemed questionable. Ironically, the spiritual leader couldn't play sports but prided himself in being an amateur martial artist. A homophobic Jamaican man a few years younger than me met me at the church. This guy was an authentic frenemy (more later), however, at this time, we were conditioned to seek opportunities to "serve the Apostle." Spiritual abuse is common too, but that's another topic to be discussed at another time.

Suddenly, a conversation about the behavior of homosexual men kicked off. Nervousness set in because I knew this was a passive-aggression directed solely at me. Another pastor and deacon side joke…again? Why do moralists always think themselves original? The native islander held his head down, but I could tell he was monitoring my body language for signs of discomfort. He had been tipped off previously by Cousin Smooth that I was gay. After all, Smooth would know because he had slowly opened a closed door and caught me swiftly rising from a compromising position with another male cousin and even helped my only gay college lover locate me. Half looking at either the Jamaican or me, Apostle made a sneering comment about down-low men who justified their need to satisfy their "freaky side," refusing to self-identify themselves as gay. He thought himself to be "in my head." I genuinely couldn't relate to his theory because I was naive to this motivation as I hadn't been able to accept it as part of myself. I said nothing, trying to maintain a poker face. My boundaries were burning, and I prayed they couldn't detect the scent.

Voice and Valor

"You have to expand yourself before you can help make others greater" (Steve Farber)

Voice and Valor

Before I joined Mount Baptist Church in my hometown, I had done praise and worship for a couple of events there, namely two choir musicals. One night, the honorees were late (as usual), so I generated spontaneous praise by dividing the bored congregation into voice parts. It catapulted the worship experience to dramatic heights before the Master/Mistress of Ceremonies stepped in.

Pastor Stevens had obviously conversed with Mitch, my landlord and the Minister of Music, about me before they found me in the choir room. Mitch, having known me since birth, must have spoken well of me. The senior leader asked me if I'd like to join the congregation. I was reluctant, but he prayed over me, rubbing my head several times as if smearing divine approval.

"Send him, Lord, send him. Send him, Lord, send him."

I agreed two Sundays later, and my ex-girlfriend, short-lived fiancée, Sabrina, soon followed. We had been the latest additions to Mitch's fourth Sunday Family and Friends Choir as well as the church's praise team. I quickly earned the respect of the congregation, and Pastor Stevens must have appointed me over the praise team. Mitch was in full agreement and seemed to appreciate my leadership until he later accused me of behaving in pride, simply because he understood hubris on a ridiculously superficial level. Someone had told him not to allow his leadership position to go to his head, and Mitch felt it his duty to pay it forward, even arbitrarily. I was, in fact, confident, excellent, healthy, independent, and interdependent.

Most leaders are unfamiliar with those like me simply because we're products of the same dangerous school of thought. Matthew Knowles stated, "I had perceived the role of leadership to consist primarily of controlling followers or subordinates. Effective leaders, I had been taught, were those who were able to get people to follow their orders." The old-school brand of leadership is draining, as any employee can attest. However, having been a tyrant in the past, received inner healing, and changed my mindset, "it gradually came to me that the highest function of leadership is releasing the energy of the people in the system and managing the processes for giving that energy direction toward mutually beneficial goals [therefore releasing] the creative energy of the people being led" (Knowles).

Knowles, the father of adult learning, tapped into the attitude of God in this manner. Jesus Christ mentored his disciples by demonstrating how to preach, heal, cast out devils, etc., sent them out two-by-two, and then asked them for feedback upon their return. Luke 10:20, NASB, quotes Jesus: *Nevertheless do not rejoice in this, that the spirits are subject to you, but rejoice that your names are recorded in heaven.* He merely adjusted their thinking as needed and sent them out again. He didn't lord over the twelve, unnecessarily scolding and firing them, but He gave them what they needed and sent them out for more practice. Why? Because Jesus knew that He would not always be with them. He enabled them to grow up.

I encourage leaders to allow their followers to mature; they will always need you at some point for wisdom and/or guidance. Jesus wasn't afraid to lose his job. It's never your job, leader, to keep butts in the seats. You'll see a steady but healthy turnover rate — one that brings back powerful, testifying disciples. This is the way the kingdom of God expands!

With the addition of my singing voice, my experienced worship leadership, keen insight, and Sabrina's soprano to the rest of the faithful members, we bonded well with Rodney, Evangelist Courtney, and married couple Bernie and Sharonda.

Mitch and I conversed periodically, and I

stepped into my new role seamlessly. In hindsight, he seemed to have mixed feelings about his rehearsing the choirs while I taught the praise singers. All he had to do was learn our music on the keys. We sang the same songs a lot during morning worship because Mitch complained about the complexities of the music I chose, and he didn't want a song list. Truth is, my involvement made Mitch have to do something he resisted: practicing. Rodney and I were classically-trained musicians, and the drummer, Kenny, also respected his craft. We tried to convince the Minister of Music to take formal lessons. He declined. God anointed the same songs we sang each Sunday, but it wasn't my volition to throw Mitch under the bus, saying his laziness and stubbornness prevented us from bringing new songs to the congregation. I even suggested he allow the keyboardist, Sean, to play for the praise team, since Mitch was content on the organ and seemed too busy to learn new music. Too bad Sean was deployed.

"Let's just flow," said Mitch. (Translation: *I don't want to be told what to do*.) My arguing a third time with Mitch would signify insubordination, so I released my frustrations to the Lord and resolved to go a different route. Determined to be a good leader, my mission was destined to expand on Mitch's design and the personal history of all my former singers.

In truth, I was beginning to burn out — been there, done that. And, wanting to avoid repeating bad leadership examples, I deliberately resisted any signs that the group was all about me. I soon got the idea to develop each member's ability to lead songs for praise and worship. Thankfully, Mitch agreed to learn the music.

In preparation for a wedding, Mitch asked Rodney to lead Donald Lawrence's song *Prayer of Jabez*, and Rodney sang it at choir rehearsal. It did not go over well, and Rodney and the rest of us knew it. Mitch, however, seemed pleased and offered my friend some supportive advice moving forward toward performing it live. Rodney returned to his seat next to me in the tenor section.

"I didn't sound too good, did I?

"No, you didn't." I knew, with my boy, I could be honest and straightforward.

"I knew it. I just don't know how to make it better."

"Personally, I think you don't sing it well because the song simply isn't... you. Just do you and stop trying to sing it like Donald Lawrence."

Voice and Valor

With that said, Rodney nodded his head at me, and he sat back, deepening himself in thought as he pondered the authenticity of my summation. Mitch had never considered this. Moving forward, I aimed to pick songs that stretched comfort zones.

For Rodney, I selected an upbeat power song that reflected his formidable fervor, didn't require him to sing a lot, capitalized on his ability to exhort, and showcased him as the authentic, passionate worshiper and masterful speaker he is. The debut at an outdoor community church event didn't go well because Mitch played the song too fast. We didn't allow ourselves to ponder if this was an act of sabotage, but a private conversation with Mitch revealed to me that Rodney, in his Minister of Music's eyes, should only sing slow songs and has never led songs for praise and worship. God had given me an eye for potential, and I was using His gift to hone my skills at developing the skills of others. Mitch didn't know this, however. The man was stuck in his thinking and only highlighted experienced singers.

We were undaunted. We featured Rodney's song, Shekinah Glory's *Awesome God*, on second Sunday. My friend gave it his all and had the congregation on their feet. Evangelist Courtney and Bernie weren't in attendance that day, so with

Voice and Valor

Sharonda on alto, Sabrina on soprano, and me holding down tenor, Rodney was free to do his thing. We all beamed from ear to ear as Rodney effectively beckoned the congregation out of spectator mode. He told them to release a loud praise each time he instructed to "put a praise right there!"

Thunderous reception! His mother was shocked and proud, despite having seen him perform on concert tympani many times and singing with the Mount Baptist Church Mass Choir. Pastor Stevens rose from his speaker's chair and gave Rodney a grand high-five. Mitch and Kenny were glad it went over so well. Rodney returned to his seat in the choir loft next to me, and all of us singers praised the featured soloist for his dynamic rendition. Ironically, Rodney later that day said that he didn't like the song the first time I allowed the team to hear it. He even said he almost bucked against me when I asked him to lead it. When I asked him why he didn't protest, Rodney cordially said that he chose instead to trust me. He recognized it as an opportunity to expand his comforts and simply give it his all. We laughed. I felt affirmed and grateful that God was glorified. Additionally, Rodney got a chance to experience the God within him. We were soon asked to sing at Kenny's mother's revival service, and Rodney *killed it* again!

For Sharonda, I picked a slightly upbeat song for her as well since she always sang slow, melodious choir songs. I showcased her soaring soprano voice in a modulating praise song, *I Will Sing Praises*. The method to my madness was to practice the song with the team two weeks before we introduced the new song to the congregation at Wednesday Bible Study. Her debut wasn't bad at all. However, Sharonda thought it was horrible; before I had formally learned the concept of "tough empathy" in my master's degree program, I was already practicing it on her. A 2009 Military Review article deemed empathy an essential leadership skill. The writer said, *In contrast to lax, easy leaders, those that practice tough empathy require firm, direct, and value-driven action that does not sacrifice standards but remains sensitive to ensuring followers grow and develop during the process.* With her husband present, I listened patiently to her feelings. I also asked her what could be done to improve her next performance of the same song, a question Sharonda dreaded. She later told me that she could tell I wasn't going to let her off the hook, despite everyone else's satisfaction, and appreciated my stance. Her personality is strong-willed, unlike my own, but when God allows me to operate in a leadership capacity, I am quite a persuasive force.

For the balance of the team, I kept in mind their experience and needs to practice other elements of worship and praise. And, again, against Mitch's wishes, I allowed Bernie to sing a slow worship song, which he performed during altar call after my initial sermon. It was anointed, and he beamed at me as God flowed through him. Evangelist Courtney was a licensed, experienced, and dynamic preacher, who greatly admired my ability to exhort, but not enough on her own. I selected a song where she could quote Psalm 24 to near completion and sing-lead us the rest of the way. She did not let us down.

Finally, Sabrina was used to the praise team framework but only sang slow melodies. I chose a familiar cut that asked the Lord to "gently rest upon our hearts." You can only imagine the sense of refreshment it brought to the early morning service.

I was in my element, enjoying helping others fulfill their potential! I was seeing my vision of working myself out of a job and realizing a team where casual onlookers would be left wondering who was the actual leader. We even appeared on television.

143

Voice and Valor

Little did I know that Sabrina was already plotting my downfall.

Voice and Valor

Valor: Great Courage in the Face of Danger, Especially in Battle

Voice and Valor

"A good woman is hard to find, and worth far more than diamonds. Her husband trusts her without reserve, and never has reason to regret it. Never spiteful, she treats him generously all her life long... Charm can mislead and beauty soon fades. The woman to be admired and praised is the woman who lives in the Fear-of-God" (Proverbs 31:10-12, 30 MSG)

Voice and Valor

The day after I had hernia surgery was the day Lady O attacked me.

"What are you gonna do now?" She crept sinisterly in to our bedroom and backed herself against the door, pushing it shut with her hands on the door knob. On the outside, my ex-wife was beautiful.

Moving my eyes from whatever television show I'd been watching, I furrowed my brow. I remember looking at her and instantly thinking, *I hope she ain't trying to pretend I've been abusing her and is now taking fake revenge. Why did I move away up north to marry this crazy ass woman?*

I was already positioned upright on our frameless bed with my back against the pillow and wall, still tender from the procedure, and wearing the original gauze. I sat under our comforter donned in sweat pants, and wearing a "wife-beater" (even though I wasn't one).

"What?"

Voice and Valor

Maintaining character, she menacingly muttered, "What you gon' do, now that you can't defend yourself?" She drew nearer and began to straddle me.

I sighed within, frustrated and annoyed. She wasn't stronger than me, and I would never have exploited this fact, however, Lady O believed she now had the upper hand. It always baffled me why certain women tested their sane men, under-estimating his strength. Women like this seem to forget that we are as strong as we are because we usually hold back when dealing with her or the kids so as to never take advantage of them. Good-natured men know they are never to use their physical advantage against females. Yet, too many women abuse their verbal superiority against gentlemen and wonder why things go south…or left.

Lady O kept trying to make eye contact with me as I periodically avoided her taunting gaze. Practicing a lower level of witchcraft, it was as if she was trying to force-feed me her lies, and I was actively trying to deny the reality of her mania. The woman amped up her disrespect and pointed her manicured index finger in my face. In self-defense, I alternated between dodging her point, turning my face, and trying to slap her finger away. Staring Lady O in the eyes, I told her to get off of me and leave me alone. We wrestled a bit with our arms and I effectively shielded myself from each violent attempt at my groin.

Careful not to tear my stitches, I did not strain. This registered as a weakness to Lady O who thought she had me. Finally, having had enough of her demented game and emasculations, I tossed her off, using her weight against her with the leverage I created with my legs. Picking herself off the floor from the other side of the bed, the thickly-built mother of two was stunned as she regained her footing. She confessed later to me that she was surprised I was still so strong.

I quickly reached for my socks, which she

batted from my grip, as she knelt in my face and continued putting me down. Bullies don't tease; they taunt. I desperately wished people, especially Sweet whom I later learned Lady O already turned against me, could have witnessed my ex-wife's dark behavior.

Battered women. I wonder if people now know that men can be battered to? Due to the shame inherent to male socialization, it wasn't in my best manly interest to tell anyone my wife was hitting me. I felt trapped and emasculated, despite the fact that I knew she couldn't overpower me. I was raised never to hit women and to walk away; however, in this case, it was far easier said than done. How many women have taken advantage of this home-training and genuinely attacked/provoked non-violent men and then cried their eyes out to the police when he defended himself? Do civil court judges know that sometimes the teary-eyed, bruised woman can actually be the *bad guy*?

All I could think was if I knocked her on her

ass, I'd have to prove myself to the authorities... and those who would close-mindedly declare "You should never put your hands on a female!" I was not in the mood to be arrested. My groin burned. I hoped the surgical mesh hadn't been compromised in the tussle. Ignoring the cold air that would seep through the holes in my comfortable sweat pants, I finally got my sneakers on after giving her a couple hard shoves that temporarily disabled her.

"Stop it! I don't know what your problem is, but I'm not gonna sit here and listen to you accuse me of something I don't do." Why had I ignored the red flags before we were wed?

"You ain't going nowhere."

I had to use my left arm to continue pushing her off me as I clamored to put on my coat with my dominant hand. Lady O resolved to blocking the bedroom door. It was humiliating to have to run away from your wife under-dressed in the snow.

"I'm tired of your abuse, Dante. You're not

going to keep hitting me and mistreating me because you don't want to be with me. I've been hit before, and I am not going to go through that again." Her speech was almost rehearsed — an ordained evangelist, irreverent of God.

I suddenly realized the scope of her scheme; Lady O was effectively trying to create scenarios which would justify her desire to divorce me. It was early winter 2004, and we just married that previous mid-autumn. Months would pass before I found out that I had wed a liar.

"Woman, you are crazy! Why are you trying to make it seem like I've been beating you? You act like that's what you want!" I motioned toward the bedroom door.

"Where you going?!" Challenging me, Lady O planted her feet.

"Move! I'm not playing this game with you. Don't make me have to hurt you to get away."

I moved forward, using as much of my
152

weight against her as possible. Restraining myself from punching my wanna-be virtuous wife in the face, I threw my shoulder against her side to pin her to the wall as I pried open the bedroom door. She began swiping at my sore spot. Being a man, I capitalized on my upper body strength while sparing force on my healing wound. I felt heat where the hernia was, attributing it to the turmoil I was enduring. Praying to God to preserve my stitches, I was forced to wrestle this Jezebel. Lady O wrapped her arms around my waist, locking her wrists with her own hands as she tried to hold me back. I struggled to loosen her grip with my hands as her back and sides smacked against the door frame.

Lady O tried this holding technique again later in Virginia, but that time she took pictures of the bruises on her wrists and back. She showed them to church members and to Sweet, building her bogus case. My character had been assassinated and people soon turned against me.

Voice and Valor

Grappling my way down the stairs, I ran for the front door which was just at the bottom. She blocked the door as I tried to remove the chain. She pounded me continually. I purposely held myself back from destroying her, so she got the upper hand. We wrestled and argued more in the living room. Truth was, fending her off while protecting my surgical wound was becoming quite tiresome. I attempted to charge past her, but she slid the wooden coffee table across our shiny wood floors to block my path. Frustrated, I stopped, cast a hateful gaze at Lady O, and took a deep breath.

Not wanting to slip or trip, I negotiated myself around the table as I made my way toward the front door. I had to get out of this house while avoiding the mounds of snow outside the back way. Lady O chained the door, providing yet another obstacle which took some time and effort to overcome, all things considered. She had turned her back to me and was covering the chain so that I couldn't unlatch it. With balled fists, I sent hammers to her hands. Lady O yelled, exaggerating her pain so the neighbors could hear. Wise to her deception, I screamed for her to move out of my way and that I was not trying to hurt her. Even at that moment, Holy Spirit was letting me know Lady O had convinced our female neighbor that I was violent.

Miraculously, I got the door opened. A very narrow vestibule separated us from the main door adjoining our duplex. I pushed her through the opening. She blocked the second door. Seconds later, I turned and ran back to our living room as Lady O threw her arm in the side doorway to prevent me from closing it.

"Move your arm!" Anchoring the door with my foot, I attempted to push her arm back toward her, safely, while trying to close the door and dart out the back. I could feel my wound burning again.

I reached through the opening and smacked Lady O on her head. The blow must have surprised her as she screamed and retracted her arm. I pushed my weight against the door, closing it shut. As I locked the door, I could hear the welcome mat slide from under her girth; she hit the floor with a thud. Ego bruised, Lady O whimpered, still trying to convince the neighbors she was under attack. I imagined her clumsily trying to remove her thick frame from the wooden surface before banging on the door.

"Let me in, Dante! Let me in!"

"I'm not doing anything to you! You're starting fights with me!"

Never have I had to vie for my character like I did with her. I darted out the back door and stood panting against the rear of the house. Perspiration and freezing temperatures aren't ideal combinations. Lady O was out front calling my name, and I could tell she wasn't sure if I had already made it to her mother's high rise around the corner, half a block away. I emerged and walked toward my mother-in-law's. Lady O followed me calmly pleading for my return to the house.

I wish I could say that was the end of the abuse in our relationship even after we got an apartment in Virginia. I thought things would be better at "home," but Lady O had already covered her tracks. She'd brainwashed Sweet, who informed her inner circle, and isolated me from any support from family and the few friends I had. To them, I had no voice because I was believed to be gay and mistreating O because of it.

One minister returned to confess to me that Lady O's spell broke over her when she realized my ex was, indeed, a habitual liar. It was bitter-sweet to be affirmed for being strong, despite enduring such enormous spiritual, emotional, physical, mental, and psycho-social abuses.

During the summer of 2017 a friend in the medical field, who read sections of this book, noted her surprise that I didn't recognize Sweet's borderline personality disorder when we read about the sickness in class. I hadn't considered it. To my knowledge, Sweet is undiagnosed, leaving only Mother Free-Spirit officially with mental issues. Of course, Sweet imagines herself superior to everyone else, masking her own insecurities and violating the privacies of others. The woman, currently 60-ish (as of 2018), believes it to be her God-given volition to know what's going on in everyone's life. I've heard rebuke someone saying, "*You* don't have no business!"

It was Fall 2003 into Spring 2005 that Lady O, in the midst of her penchant for vicariousness, projections, and unhealed issues with her abusive father, continued to cause me pain.

Voice and Valor

"False shame is associated with false condemnation as in the double bind form of false shaming; "he brought what we did to him upon himself" (Wikipedia authors)

Voice and Valor

"Jamaica, come with me! Dante done lost his dog-bite mind and hit O!"

Yes, I "hit" her in front of Sweet and her friend, Meg. Sweet was summoned via cell phone by Lady O, to whom I was still married during the spring of 2004. My heart was broken, and I wanted to break my wife's jaw.

The events that led up to my assault on Lady O had been mounting. On our wedding day, instead of mutually feeding each other, she shoved cake in my face. An observing Apostle Pimp and Jamaica, who no doubt put her up to it, laughed. I always felt these men were jealous of my positive qualities. And, although they knew I was a good brother, they sorely resented me because I wasn't tough enough for them. They believed I was gay (despite my having been "clean" for years). Therefore, in their minds, any form of humiliation would serve as a means of payback or toughening, depending on their whim... Jesus's name, of course.

160

Voice and Valor

Shame can be layered. Isn't that right, Reader? They'd be the prototypical Christians that like to evangelize and antagonize at the same time. Lady O, too, thought of me as weak due to my non-macho, clean-cut personality.

We had a small wedding reception at my childhood home. Onlookers watched the Lady smear decorated batter on my nose and mouth. The look on her face reflected sheer evil satisfaction. Keen and embarrassed, I was aware of the plotters, glimpsed at the co-conspirators, resented them, and turned a sneer back at O. I adjusted the grip on my handful of cake. Trying to maintain her air of sophistication, my Jezebel-like bride saw her own doom in my gaze and took a small step backward.

As she begged and threw up her arm to protect herself.

"Dante, don't do it! Dante, I'm telling you...!" I made sure she saw my cake-filled hand as she turned her head this way and that. Oh, how I

Voice and Valor

longed to give her face and hair a sweet makeover!

Apostle Pimp spoke up, "Danteee, don't do that to your wife." He was trying to control me and make me allow myself to be disrespected.

Manipulation, even the spiritual kind, can be subtle. I figured he believed I deserved humiliations like these as payment for being non-heterosexual. As if I did anything to him! He longed for the day I would cry out to him for deliverance and prayer.

Toxic shame causes church hurt, no matter who wants to deny or minimize its reality.

At that time, I was a people-pleaser and on-the-fence blind follower of Pimp, our "spiritual father/leader." So, I decided to fake pump one last threat at a falsely vindicated Lady O. She flinched and let her arms down, wearing a disdainful, annoyed expression much like one a woman wears when she's having to tolerate a punk. I knew all this and despised the shame. My self-confidence was far below the level it is today.

Voice and Valor

Mind you, at this stage in my life I sincerely wanted to be "delivered" from the struggle with the "homosexual spirit." Contrary to popular religious teachings, I don't presently believe there is a gay demon, yet I was headed by an immature and homophobic, radical Pentecostal preacher who targeted me for his resumé of deliverances. He and others took advantage of my kind nature (forgetting gentleness and kindness are one of the fruits of the Spirit). They took advantage of my wanting camaraderie as opportunities toward deliverance.

Apostle also knew I played the flute, was a good boy growing up, and was non-athletic. The funny thing was, Apostle Pimp, himself, was awkward at sports, but he over-compensated for this damning social quality by bringing up his martial arts training and promoting hyper-heterosexual, misogynistic ideologies. Nearly every woman in our small congregation had been accused of sleeping with him at some point. Sex rumors plagued our assembly; our church was just as anointed as O was insane.

That night we had people speak
prophetically over us at my request. Admittedly,
there was no fire from Heaven, a reminder of the
unlit candles at our wedding. Sweet sang her go-to
"the Lord will place you on hind's feet" prophecy
as if no one had heard her use that on other people
in the past. Our co-pastor and a senior minister,
Mary and Elmer, gave us an exhortation to be
patient with adjusting to our new lives together. She
and Elmer had been unhappy for years, but her
spoiled past, questions about her husband's
sexuality, and financial struggles plagued them
toward a recent divorce. Apostle Pimp, twice-
divorced and dating Prophet Joy, decided to conduct
a crash marital counseling session at the reception.
Remember, he later married Joy, divorced her, and
tried to get back with his second wife. It was
grueling to endure. Yeah, crazy, right?

True to his temperamental penchant for self-
appointment, Pimp knew he was unfit to council us.

Voice and Valor

He publicly qualified himself under the guise that although he could not tell us what *to* do, he could tell us what *not* to do in a marriage. Humility was never his strong suit.

Moving forward, Lady O and I had an uncomfortable wedding night. She and I had had sex before she purchased our rings. Superficial church teachers who swear that sex before marriage causes marital turmoil would love to pat themselves on this "false opportunity." Regardless, our case was destined to fall apart; I was in between employment, having relocated after being laid-off from a seasonal job with the IRS. Would you believe she had me to get down on one knee after she rushed to get the rings? Lady O and her mother (who soon endeared me) made fun of the fact that *a woman paid* when we went to get the marriage license.

Looking back on these instances, as I write this section in June 2018, allowed me to realize how much abuse I endured. My history was frocked with abandonment and a lack of emotional support, so each time I spoke up, I wasn't respected.

We had sex doggy-style that night, and she came. But there was no intimacy. Her mind was on someone else.

The night before we wed, I had ignored all the future drama God was showing me. I, a man of integrity, stubbornly held to my commitment to marry her and didn't want the embarrassment of canceling a wedding. I felt that since I was a genuine, godly man and not a pedophile, Lady O and her children were in safe hands. Years later, I remain repentant of my pride and rebellion.

The only comfort is that I know I was meant to meet her son, Xavier. The Lord reminded me of a dream I had of him no more than a year before we met in person — kinda like "ordered steps" and deja vu. She emotionally and physically abused him. And, in that dream, I saw that in his eyes as he watched helplessly as I climbed into a dark-colored

166

van. While sleeping I saw myself carrying the last of my possessions as some woman yelled at me from behind. Xavier stood in the driveway, wishing I didn't have to move away but careful not to let on how he felt. If he had, X would have to deal with his mother's wrath after I was gone.

On my wedding night, the Lord told me this union was doomed.

Reader, the list is expansive...

1. Lady O picked a lot of fights. She tried to make me feel bad for spanking Xavier for playing with fire at his grandmother's house.

2. This woman railroaded me twice into O-biased, pre-arranged marital counseling sessions with busy-bodyish women that she herself bad-mouthed to me in private.

3. Turns out as well that Lady O was still obsessed with her fire-fighter ex-boyfriend, Bryson, who married another woman behind her back. Unwittingly, I was her revenge.

Again, these two finally married, her third husband within four years.

4. Did I mention she had two abortions during our marriage? She told me the first was a miscarriage. I went against my better judgment and ignored my conscience. It felt weird because I was expecting some kind of proof, but she manipulated me with her abdominal pain and need for rest.

5. Early into our marriage, Lady O suddenly didn't want to engage in oral sex, self-righteously calling it sodomy, or have intercourse anymore. I made sexual advances for a short while but then refused to continue begging for something I was supposed to get regularly. She told Apostle Pimp and Sweet I wasn't asking her for sex. They, of course, being over-simplistic and ignorant as hell, attributed this to my struggle with that "homosexual spirit."

6. I believe she was secretly sleeping with her obsession, Bryson, while we were married. After all, Lady O's best friend, who respected me, later confessed that O had been conversing with Bryson throughout the day leading up to the hour of our wedding ceremony.

She even tried to persuade the OB/GYN to deceive me.

"What, you want me to lie for you?"

Lady O went quiet and cast a nervous side-eye at me. I sat, staring off into space, angry, ashamed, and feeling like an idiot. She and I routinely discussed the fact that sex is beneficial for child birthing and how women usually crave intercourse during pregnancy. Lady O annoyed me with repetitious declarations that her hormones were acting up. The medical professional was wise to her plot and called her out in my presence. Despite the circumstances, I did not want to air our dirty

169

Voice and Valor

laundry in public with a screaming match. Our ride home was a pregnant silence. I knew that no matter what I said, she would retaliate with bullshit, plain and simple. To keep from choking her out, I swallowed my rage and began biding my time.

Weeks before Sweet witnessed me strike Lady O, I had already moved back "home" with my disloyal aunt, mother, and Muscle. Sweet interfered and got O and I back together. Despite my differences with Aunt Sweet, she still had a very special place in my heart at that time. I held onto the false belief that she would eventually see Lady O's true nature.

My wife and I got an apartment on the south side of Norfolk when yet another argument surfaced at the storage center. As usual, Lady O wanted to run the show, but since I had put up with so much of her nonsense on her turf, I wasn't about to be further emasculated in my own hometown.

She had other plans.

Voice and Valor

Lady O pretended to be in danger as I stood putting her in her place while she sat defiantly behind the wheel of her SUV. My car was parked a space away from hers. She threatened to call my aunt to rescue her. O wanted Sweet to see me worked up. She dialed. I heard her falsely accusing me, making herself seem innocent. I ripped the phone from Lady O's grip and told her not to be calling my family when we're settling an argument. I never called *her* mother on her. Lady O resented me because her mom had begun taking my side against her daughter's because O's history was frocked with fights, confusion, and deceit. Her mom also knew about Bryson.

"Give me back, my phone, Dante!"

Through the phone, I heard Sweet yell, "Leave her alone, Dante!"

"Aunt Sweet, stay out of this. Lady O and I can handle this on our own."

O let out a pretty convincing "Nooo!"

Voice and Valor

"O, I am on my way. Dante, don't you do anything to her!!!"

I was livid... beyond comprehension.

I threw the phone at O's lap and stood by my car fuming.

Soon, Sweet emerged from Meg's car, and immediately started scolding me.

Overcome with fury at my wife's ability to turn my blood relative against me, I walked over to Lady O.

"What the hell is your problem?!"

I mushed her chin... much less than what I *wanted* to do.

Lady O yelled, "Dante, leave me alone!"

Sweet screamed, "Oh, you're in for it now! Let's see if you can handle Jamaica."

Jamaica was a two-faced ally and had been my best man. He was much shorter than me but had the reputation of being a rough and tough thug prior to his conversion to Christ. I envied the respect he received from our peers and Apostle Pimp and heard many of Jamaica's stories, or *tall tales*. This, of course, intimidated me a bit and qualified him in everyone's mind to beat me up and set me straight. He had been sitting in the back of Meg's vehicle. Homophobic and over-confident, he flexed his arms and advanced toward me.

"Look, man. You don't be putting your hands on a female!"

Betrayed and furious, I defied my usual clean-cut reputation. I marched toward him and shoved him so hard that he later told me he almost threw up. The thug had recently eaten.

"Get out of my way!"

God allowed this moment to teach me the most important part of winning valor: the mind. I had determined within myself that day that even though he had more experience than me in the streets, I wasn't going down easily. My aim was to win some self-respect no matter what. Needless to say, Jamaica had nothing for me after my attack. He knew I wasn't about to back down as he had expected. He stood stunned.

I stepped on and said through bitter tears, "Sweet, how dare you take her side against your own nephew?!"

Not waiting for a reply, I turned away from the shocked Sweet and Meg, shot Jamaica a warning glance, got back in my car, and sped away. I didn't look at Lady O, most likely because I may would have done more to her.

False shame… In Sweet's mind, I was behaving like her drunken father who used to beat his wife. The truth? Grandad and I are not the same men. Sweet was projecting onto me the blame that was do her father and the punishments she felt should have been served upon him.

Readers, please get healed and/or counseling

174

about painful, past issues. When we don't we can't see clearly, and we're what Jesus was saying that we're ill-equipped to remove the speck of sawdust out of our neighbor's eye because of the plank in our own (Matthew 7:3).

Jamaica, Pimp, and Elder Anne came to me at separate times in the future, telling me Sweet attempted to get O to press charges against me that night to which my aunt valiantly declared, "And, I will testify!"

Of course, when I confronted Sweet a year or so later (when I found out) to let her know that three independent witnesses said the same thing, she denied it. She could never admit when she was wrong. Busted, therefore untrusted.

Voice and Valor

"Standing up for yourself can be really challenging if you're used to letting others have their way or you're a people pleaser. When you trim yourself down to suit everyone else, it can all be too easy to whittle yourself away; learning to stand up for yourself is a way of ensuring other people respect you and don't try to push you around or manipulate you. Unlearning the old habits of self-effacement and gaining confidence to stand up for yourself won't happen overnight, but the journey to improvement starts with the first step." (Wikihow)

Voice and Valor

It was very near dusk when I left Sweet, Meg, Jamaica, and Lady O at the storage center. I drove around town, desperate for clarity and full of adrenaline. My car was loaded with belongings to go in to the apartment for O and me: stuff for us and things belonging to Xavier and Alexandria.

I decided to go to the church in order to seek council from Apostle Pimp. Once I left his presence, I was surprised to see that a large group of our congregants had amassed themselves in front of the building and across the street. I walked to my car and saw Sweet standing across the street with her arm around an upset O, who, by the way, couldn't look at me. Jamaica stood by Sweet's side like a bodyguard and witness.

In disbelief, I got in to my parked car. I was embarrassed, falsely accused, and needing Jamaica to make good on his previous agreement to help me move so I could tell him what happened between O and me so he and I could squash this beef.

Voice and Valor

"Jamaica, you ready?"

He shuffled his feet a bit and raised his chin. "Nah, I'm not."

I sighed. I knew this was partly about the shame over my homosexual past being used against me again. Also now, who would want to be seen with the "wife-beater," especially after you've just lost a squabble with that same man. No doubt, Jamaica didn't share that information if he'd been talking junk about it all before I arrived. I had forgotten I'd "won" because fighting wasn't how I identified myself.

I turned on my car. Sweet knew I was heading home to meet Uncle Muscle because he'd previously agreed to allow me to use his SUV to move my family's possessions.

"Be ready!"

I had no idea what she meant until Muscle answered the door of my childhood home.

Voice and Valor

"Your aunt [Sweet] told me you put your hands on that girl! What are you doing putting your hands on her like that?"

I could tell he was building himself up to try to hit me. He'd known me since my birth that I wasn't a fighter. Muscle was the burly protector of our home, but he also has a learning disability. Still, I was steely in my resolve, ready to fight and reason with him.

"Why is everyone so quick to take her side all the time? You know me, Uncle. You've known me much longer than you've known her, and you never once asked to hear my side of the story!"

He heard me but was conflicted. Sweet, a witch in her own right, cast a spell on him. It was like watching a man fighting his own conscience against a demonic entity.

Muscle advanced toward me. "You still put your hands on her!"

"Oh, so you want to fight me now? And you

haven't even heard me out?"

He stood still and said, "I ought to."

Passionate in my stance, I looked at him and said, "Alright, but you best know I didn't hit her like Sweet made it sound. I was provoked because O turned my own aunt against me!"

Muscle was just about to step toward me when Apostle Pimp and Jamaica jumped out of a car behind me. The new arrivals had seen us screaming at each other. My uncle saw them. I stepped a safe distance away from him and braced myself to have to fight these two as well. It was as if the whole world turned against me.

Everyone experiences abandonment, betrayal, and rejection during points in their life, but here I was experiencing them all at the same time! I still need inner healing from this instance as I write. I thank God for having kept my mind.

"Son?"

Voice and Valor

I heard an unfamiliar gentleness in Apostle's voice. He was walking slowly toward me with his hands slightly raised, resembling a hostage negotiator. Jamaica walked even slower beside him as if afraid to come close to me too quickly.

I said, "Oh, so ya'll came to fight me too?"

I developed a *fuck-all-ya'll!* mindset. Reader, I was ready to scrap for my life and mortally wound the unlucky one(s)! And, they could see it.

"Son--"

"--Stop calling me that!" I growled. "You're not my father, and you're not on my side! No one is fucking listening to me!"

Even gentler, Apostle paused. "I'm not here to try to do anything to you. We're just here to check on you." They knew Sweet had "sicked" her bulldog brother on their own nephew. Shameful!

Side note: Jezebel, whose name means

Voice and Valor

unhusbanded, is synonymous with the spirit of
control, witchcraft, false authority, and, among
other things, killing prophets. According to Dr. N.
Cindy Trimm, Jezebel is the wife of Satan. She
would routinely employ the biblical sons of Belial,
the entity behind gang-like activities, to do her dirty
work. No wonder Jamaica and Muscle were so
willing to disregard my clean history of violence
and readily attack me. Sweet exaggerates crises and
can work anyone up if they're not wise.

However, I could see the new arrivals' calm
body language and the sincerity in their eyes.

Muscle countered, "Naw, Dante, I ain't
about to let no woman-beater use my truck. You're
in the public eye now. Don't you understand that?"
The way he talked, you'd think I recently appeared
on national television.

"So, just because I preached here publicly
one time, I'm *in* the public eye?"

Muscle must have felt a little stupid after I

said that, but he couldn't shake the spell completely. This would be the same husky, solid man with whom I would be trying to climb in to a window of our foreclosed family home. Unaccustomed to seeing me being physical, Muscle was shocked that I could catch his stocky build, could cradle him in my arms, and could ask him if he was alright to prevent him from falling to the ground.

"All I'm saying is no. Move your own stuff some other way!"

He walked back into the house. Was he spooked and now afraid to fight me and/or the other two? I don't care.

Think he ever apologized to me? I don't hold it against him, however. I've had to learn to forgive without apology a number of times in my life.

"I've never seen you like this before." Apostle Pimp made his way to my side, folded his arms almost proudly. After all, it takes a hell of a lot to get me mad enough to fight.

"Yeah, man." Jamaica walked up.

I eyed him but allowed my adrenaline to level off.

I said, "All I want to do is be heard and feel like my reputation will speak for itself. No one knows how evil Lady O can be. That woman has a side to her ya'll haven't seen."

As the story goes, O and I moved in together and lived unhappily thereafter.

Jamaica and I made amends, but I knew he still thought himself better than me because of hetero-superior ideals. Like most marginalized parties, I simply went learned to live with it. He knew he couldn't touch me spiritually or intellectually. Males, however, are socialized to rigidly prioritize hyper-masculinity above all else.

He lived with O and me for a short period later in our 1½ years of marriage. Jamaica wasn't

working at the time and cleaning out the house his
mother was selling. After job hunting, he was
spending a lot of time with Xavier, teaching him
how to be a man. Jamaica felt I was unfit for the
job, a logical fallacy common to homophobia and,
again, hetero-superiority.

Lady O played on this and flirted with him
once in my presence, trying to make me believe that
they were having an affair. They, in fact, were not
messing around because I knew Jamaica wasn't that
type. He'd previously confided in me that he could
tell O really liked "bad boys."

Lady O, on one of my days off, pleaded to
me citing sexual frustration and unhappiness and
how if a man doesn't tend to his garden (like Eden),
then a serpent can sneak in and deceive the woman.
I shook my head at her warped biblical
interpretation and told her if she wanted to step out
on me then to go ahead. God won't hold me
responsible because I have done everything in my
power to be a good husband and father. She was

trying to insinuate Jamaica, but I later realized the real serpent had been Bryson. Who knew, but God, how many times she met with Bryson while I was at work and the kids at school?

Honestly, I knew everything that was going on in my house. One day I pulled Jamaica aside and reminded him that he wasn't X's father. He backed off.

Soon, I had begun staying out late after work to avoid the chaos at home. However, her deception played with my mind while I was away. Even though I knew there was no disrespect on Jamaica's part intellectually, O had stirred my jealousy. It was the second night around 3 am that I decided to surprise Lady O with a confrontation.

I burst into the house and flicked on the lamp. Jamaica was fast asleep on a pallet on our living room floor. Marching toward the steps I barked, "Jamaica, upstairs now!"

I paused as the groggy dwarf rubbed his

Voice and Valor

eyes, "What's going on, man?"

"Nothing, I just need you up here!"

I heard him huff, but he complied.

The door to the bedroom in which O and I slept was open, so I flicked on the wall light switch and startled Lady O out of her sleep. She sat up, using the comforter to cover her night gown.

"O, wake up! Are you two sleeping together?"

Jamaica was still half asleep, shocked, and said no. His body language was completely sincere.

"Dante, what's going on, man?"

I watched as O sulked in silence.

"Lady O tried to insinuate that you two had something going on."

Check! O looked even more guilty.

"Naw, man! Naw! I would never disrespect you like that, feel me? Ya'll here helping me out.

Voice and Valor

I'm a man of God, son, feel me?"

Check mate.

"I just wanted to confront you both in front of each other and get the truth."

Lady O, the habitual liar, had to have felt even smaller than ever.

Soon thereafter, Jamaica moved out because my house was becoming more and more like the movie, *War of the Roses.* He told me that he confided in Apostle Pimp and a select few others that Lady O had been the culprit in my marriage all along.

Finally, some acknowledgment! "Man, I'm so sorry for everything I ever said negative about you. You are in a tough situation, and I got your back, man, if anyone comes at me with some foolishness about you. I've seen it for myself. I told people it was never you, but it was O."

Soon, others who were deceived by O came

Voice and Valor

forward and began telling me they either never or no longer believed I was abusive.

Sometimes, valor requires nothing from you. Reader, know that God hears your cries and bottles your tears. He will fight for you, too. One of His names is Jehovah Gibbor!

I felt vindicated by this support, but, as you can imagine, I would have appreciated loyalty from my closest relatives a lot sooner. They taught me that when the chips were down, they would not be supportive.

Growing up, I never would have thought I'd have to stand up for myself against my own wife.

Sometime after Lady O moved away, I took a moment to talk with Spicy, Sweet's twin, defender, and confidante, about how hurt I was that they didn't believe me and had taken the word of a stranger to our family. I offered her an opportunity to acknowledge her wrong. On behalf of Sweet and herself, Spicy "apologized" with, "She deceived us all."

"That's all you have to say?"

"Yes, she fooled us all."

Voice and Valor

"Hitting a woman is not something a real man does, and that's true whether or not an act of violence happens in the public eye, or, far too often, behind closed doors. Stopping domestic violence is all of [our] responsibility [and we must] put a stop to it" (Britni)

Voice and Valor

"I knew you had hit your wife," Sabrina sneered immediately after I slapped her face.

Still angry and shaking, I ignored her accusation referring to Lady O but countered, "Excuse me? Did you not just put your hands on me?" I could still feel the blow the woman gave my chest as she drove her car.

Sabrina was the first woman I dated after my divorce. She and I had been considering marriage just before I learned Spicy got wind that one of our cousins, Celeste, happened to have been Sabrina's cubicle neighbor at work. According to Sabrina's testimony, Sweet, Spicy, and Celeste had been gossiping about my sexuality, but Sweet later told me that only Sabrina was the one tearing down my manhood. That was the reason Sweet said she didn't like the idea of Sabrina and me getting married. *Bitter, immature, gossipy, and messy females — each of them.*

Sabrina was a member of the praise team,

which I led. It just so happened that she had gone to the same school my best friend, Rodney, who also sang with us. He once confided in me that she was crazy, even in high school. I soon learned that Mitch, who fathered Sweet's second baby and whom I'd known since I was a child, had actually known Sabrina for years, and that she was more dominant than her identical twin sister.

Mitch suddenly emerged from his room visibly angry at me. "It makes no sense, the two of you passing licks."

"Passing licks? First of all, we aren't children, and don't take that tone with me when you haven't even heard my side of the story."

"Sabrina told me you hit her."

"So now you're *automatically* mad at me? I was just as upset as she was before she threw her arm against my chest... but I never would have hit her. She hit me first, and this was not the first time she's hit me." At our pre-marital counseling session, Sabrina had been forthright in confessing to Pastor Stevens that she struck me when she was mad. He sternly told her never to hit (even while playing). She did it anyway.

Mitch hadn't been privy to this conversation until I told him.

"You can't be putting your hands on females, Dante!"

"Excuse me?!" I was becoming annoyed. "Did you not just hear me say that Sabrina hit me first?!"

Knowing the psychology of male socialization, I was well aware of the vehemence men dredge up at the notion of hearing of and/or witnessing a man assaulting a woman as well as the deaf ear they turn to men who've hit females. One of the triumphs of social media is YouTube's having availed compilations of women who persistently provoked men until, finally, guys decided to defend themselves. Most violent, antagonizing females accuse the male of being a punk before and after he hits her while she completely ignores her own behavior. Rarely do onlookers, especially the aggressive female's best friend, understand the floored girl's tragic flaw. Women aren't usually stronger than men. His previous restraint stimulated her false sense of bravery, however, and her audience and the high her mouth was giving her egged her on.

Cousin Lydia told me that she teaches her daughter and sons that some, not all, women take advantage of the fact that most men are taught since childhood never to hit a girl/female "because she is a girl/female." I share this tutelage with my students in the public schools when I witness young girls being overly aggressive with boys and are shocked when he retaliates or tries with all his might not to take revenge. Teaching boys not to hit girls is only half right, thanks to the above-quoted Britni.

Mitch paused. I could tell how brainwashed he was by society as he sighed away the notion that

Voice and Valor

I wasn't in a position to "just walk away." In the past, I'd "walked away," but this time I couldn't, one — because I was in a moving car, and two — because I was tired of Sabrina getting away with her aggressiveness.

"You saw she had an attitude before we left. We get more than an hour away, and Sabrina suddenly starts calling me a *gay blade, faggot, homo,* and asking me accusingly *What do you want with me?* She was saying things like *That's why your own family be talking about you like they do and how you used to play Wonder Woman as a little boy. What kind of a boy does that? Yeah, Celeste and them told me. I don't deal with no weak men!*"

What four-year-old knows about being "all boy," as people say?

Truth is, I was incredibly ashamed. Knots were in my stomach, and emotional pangs hit my head. But I had to continue talking to Mitch… or someone.

Voice and Valor

"I asked her what her problem was, especially after I already confessed to her months ago about my past, but I hadn't gone back that way in years." It was genuinely a thing of the past in my mind... and God too no longer held it against me, for that matter. Right, Christians?

As an aside: I remember the night Sabrina mysteriously revealed to me that three of my family members — Sweet, Spicy, and Celeste — betrayed me. To get her away, she and I drove to a local park and sat on the swings. It was dark, and we were alone. Not one to lie, I confessed to having experimented with literally a few boys in the past (able to count them on one hand) and girls at different points in my life. However, I believed God "delivered" me. No one knew all the times I had begged away, fasted and cried to be rid of, and suppressed my same-sex desires. I even immediately regretted giving in to them right after performing homosexual acts, wondering how my family (and friends) would feel about me if they found out.

Human opinions, to be honest, outweighed how I felt God thought. I was a bona fide people-pleaser, raised to be that way since birth. I still repented to the Heavenly Father though and could hardly wait for the guilty feelings to fade away. Looking back, this was the way I determined I was back to my spiritual self (the effects of the kryptonite had worn off); God had forgiven me and I could stand as a man and against the devil again.

Sabrina, however, sat there listening, twisting her hair into a braid. I could tell she wasn't "hearing" me. Ranting and feeling superior, the self-righteous woman's frown decorated her nasal voice, "But what do you want with me, Tay? You want a man. Have you been with Mitch?"

I knew she'd go there sooner or later.

"No, nothing ever happened between me and Mitch. I don't want to be with a man. I knew what I did in my past was wrong, so I repented and

198

stopped years ago. And, it wasn't like I was living some *lifestyle*." I now resent the targeted use of that word. *Lifestyle*. "Why are you judging me for something from my past? I can't do anything about my history. I love you, have been faithful to you, was to my ex-wife, and I only want to be with you."

"Judging you? Ain't nobody *'juuudging'* you. That's the first thing y'all wanna say when someone is calling y'all out about that sin. Ain't nobody judging you."

I raised my eyebrow contemplating her usage of "y'all." Sounded like "you people." Hetero-supremacy, indeed, manifests in various forms.

The attitude of her reply was unwarranted. I was being vulnerable, speaking transparently and calmly. She seemed as though she was responding aloud to my prick at to her conscience, as if battling with God, logic, or simply compulsively repeating a segment from previous discussions about the subject.

Knowing Sabrina was high-strung, intense, and a highly emotionally immature prophet, I resolutely countered her outburst. She was grappling with obeying the biblical notion to "judge not" lest she be judged with the same scrutiny and fervor she exhibited. I suggested she ask herself, since all I had done was in the past, did she or did she not believe that when a man is in Christ, then old things pass away and all things became new?

Tired of this continual battle, I became a little sarcastic. "I'm trying to move forward in God. Why am I feeling like I am asking the world for forgiveness for something I did in my past? I didn't even sin against them!"

Not wanting to admit my savvy and the fact that I got her, Sabrina merely frowned, rolled her eyes, and stared back at me in silence as she braided her hair. She had very large eyes and an annoying gaze at times. We slumped there on the swings a

Voice and Valor

while before I pulled her up for a hug and kiss. She giggled, though her mind kept tumbling. We left the park on decent terms.

Yet here I was days later, age 29, explaining myself to Mitch, another bisexual man. I only indulged him with my story in desperation for emotional support.

I pleaded. "Mitch, you have known me since I was a kid. You know I was never a fighter and that if I was in a fight, I didn't start it! I would never hit a woman..."

My inner vow had been betrayed. I remember feeling like a liar, one who had just contradicted himself. Logic vindicated me, and though I tried, I felt inept to justify myself. I instantly remembered all the men I shut out, having immediately judged them for hitting women. I remembered the men I called punks and sissies for wielding their violent hands. I recalled a group of church men with whom I caravanned to an abusive

man's house to defend the honor of one of our
sisters.

"…but this woman has hit me four separate
times in the past." I was certain of what I spoke,
hoping Mitch's quiet attention meant understanding.
"I was just as mad as she was. I kept my hands to
myself, so why couldn't she? When she hit me, I
had to finally let her see a side of me that she'd
never seen before!"

Prior to her striking me in the chest, Sabrina
had gotten louder as I protested her vindictiveness.
It was just as uncalled-for as it was demeaning,
emasculating, humiliating, maddening, and unfair.

Recalling the events to Mitch, I became
animated and used my hands like puppets facing
each other.

"As she took it to one level, I matched it and
took it up a notch…" I raised one puppet higher.
"…then she matched me and took it to the next
level of ferocity. I matched her and then took it to

202

the hilt."

Still trying to sustain my dignity and give her a dose of her own medicine, I reminded Sabrina of the time she told me she invited her twin sister and a couple of her female friends into the bathroom with her. Sabrina had gotten sick and, being the over-maternal creature she is, took it upon herself to teach them about yeast infections. Had I told her *I'd* invited *men* to watch me take a bath... you already know. She also had one or more relationships with married men but conveniently ignored her indiscretions and judged mine as worse.

Hetero-superiority.

By this time, I was voicing the puppets with growing intensity, opening and closing my hands even slower as I drifted my hand back and forth from the Sabrina puppet. I moved them as if puppet Dante was seconds away from devouring her.

I told Mitch, "I laid into her, calling her every name I'd wanted to call her every time I

203

walked away from her nastiness and hitting me."

I finally started calling her a lesbian. I repeated the slur at least five times, slower than the times before it, trying to dig the words into her flesh-- all this while she was driving. When I kept chanting "lesbian" and ignored her sudden, calm requests for me to stop calling her that, Sabrina then swung her arm and fist into my torso to shut me up. Shocked and beyond angry, I looked down at my chest, then at her, and back-handed her right cheek. Knowing my own strength, I deliberately exhibited self-control and hit Sabrina hard and fast enough to surprise her but not hurt her.

She swerved and recovered. "Did you just hit me? Uh huh, Imma get that ass, you faggot ass punk you! That's gon' be the last time you hit a woman."

Bringing you, Reader, back to the top, she said, "I knew you had hit your wife!"

Like most abusive people, she used sensitive

Voice and Valor

information I had confided in her against me.
Reasons like these are why many men/husbands
don't trust their women/wives. When women get
angry, they fight unfairly.

Sabrina pulled in to the nearest gas station
and put me out. Angry at this horribly wrong
treatment, I yelled, "How will I get home? You
started this!"

"I don't care! I'll call Mitch or somebody to
come get that ass."

I got out and closed her car door. Tears
welled up in my eyes. My adrenaline sky-rocketed
as my heart beat faster and faster, knowing I'd be in
for some physical altercation for my integrity and
not knowing how I was going to get home. Sabrina
called someone on her mobile and watched me as I
stood in the convenient store. I glanced angrily at
her a few times through the windows as a million
thoughts were running through my head. I had no
cell phone at that time and no money to make a pay

Voice and Valor

phone call.

Finally, she waved me back to the car. We sped away and rode in silence for over an hour on the way back to Mitch's house. She parked and followed me in to the house, disrespecting me because it technically wasn't mine. I knew I'd have to fight her and attract unnecessary drama to keep her away. The only person I knew she later confessed her evil to was the seasoned Mrs. Stone, who told me that Sabrina said she was scared. The older woman was surprised when I told her the younger female had followed me in to the house after our fight and long ride back.

I went upstairs to my room, confident that my integrity was intact and ready to tell Mitch. By the time I came back downstairs after hearing the front door close, I went in to the den of the house. That's when the biased, weak-willed Mitch emerged. Talking to other men about this, giving them the same story you're reading, only seemed to isolate me further as even Rodney came off unsupportive… at first.

I wish I could say that when I privately told Pastor Stevens, man-to-man, what had precipitated between Sabrina and I that he uttered a word besides "thanks for letting me know." She didn't show up to sing for bible study that Wednesday — I hadn't spoken to her since Monday when it all happened. I wish I could say that our spiritual leader respected me and didn't eventually take her side. I wish I could tell you, Reader, that he hadn't told her to box the possessions I had left at her house and bring them to his church office. I asked him by whose authority this was arranged.

"Mine!"

I lowered my head and looked at him credulously, "And? Who are you?"

"The pastor."

"Oh…" I casted a sarcastic glare at him as if to ask, "that's your excuse?" I was growing tired of the church.

Voice and Valor

I wish I didn't have to walk a box of personal belongings to my car in the casual sight of church members. I wish I could say that Sabrina wasn't one of many women whom Pastor Stevens favored in domestic situations. I wish I wasn't among a list of men who were forced to count their losses and endure the subsequent church gossip. Stevens appointed Sabrina an elder within weeks after I left his church.

And my ex-landlord, Mitch? Years after I discontinued my church membership there, Mitch surprise-called me one morning apologizing for not listening to me when I was trying to tell him about crazy Sabrina.

"Dante," he confessed, "when the news first got out, your name was dirt. Now that I and some others have experienced her attitude myself, if you did hit her, I can see why. Man, please forgive me. I can now see why some men end up hitting women because Sabrina will make you want to hurt her."

Voice and Valor

Strong, noble men throughout history have had to genuinely defend themselves against the so-called "weaker sex." How many men have been unjustly sentenced to anger-management classes? Maybe you know one. My boy Rodney is another man who had to "put his hands on" an overly aggressive female, my father as well. Anyone ever seen the movies *A Thin Line Between Love and Hate* or *Fatal Attraction*, or analyzed the restaurant smack in *Tyler Perry's The Family That Preys*? Ever heard the other side of the conflict on *Netflix's Chris Brown: Welcome to My Life*? "Bad guys" aren't always guys.

Voice and Valor

"A child needs the presence of both parents. For a boy child to break his mother bonding, he needs a father to bond with. Bonding involves spending time together, sharing feelings, warmth, touching, and displaying desire to be with one another"
(John Bradshaw)

Voice and Valor

"I told her that if you're as much like me as they say you are, then you didn't hit her but restrained her. And, if you did hit her, then you didn't do it to hurt her. You most likely hit her to get away from her. That's what I would have done."

The moment my biological father uttered these words to me was, perhaps, one of the most ironic moments of my life. He and I had just reunited. How was it that Regular Lee Alone, my absentee hero, was able to single-handedly affirm my character to Holiday, my half-sister's mother? Lady O had systematically cast her spell on everyone I knew while I went to work each day. According to Regular and Holiday, during the latter part of my marriage, Lady O showed Holiday bruises on her back and wrists. My ex-wife had been planting seeds of doubt about my character, telling people I was beating her to justify her secret, selfish desire to divorce me. Each of you, Readers, know how she got the wounds. Holiday told Lady O that which I wished Sweet, Spicy, and everyone else

Voice and Valor

who's known me since boyhood had said in my defense: "I've never known Dante to have beaten on any of his ex-girlfriends. What did you do to him?"

True to her over-protective nature, however, Holiday moved on to punctuate her inquiry declaring I'd be a dead brother if I had ever decided to hit my sister. I imagine this was her "just in case." And even though I felt the last part was unnecessary, I considered the source and took it for what it was worth. Holiday should have shown me respect by first telling me what my ex-wife had done, but I was glad she told my dad.

Regular Lee Alone, before this writing, heard rumors about my sexuality but never treated me as if he believed them. He was, however, fascinated by my long memory. Living with him a short while, I told him I remembered the day I'd been circumcised. I was just two years old when my father carried me upstairs to Grandma and Grandad's room. He instinctively knew how to carry me, with my super-uncomfortable wound

Voice and Valor

facing away from his own body and my legs draped over his strong forearm as I held onto his shirt refusing to let go. He told me I didn't want to come to anyone but him, including my beautiful mother and grandma. Free-Spirit was close by, my two parents in relationship before chaos destroyed their connection. Early in my father's army career, he would spend weekends at the Painter house.

Regular made it to the top of the stairs where Grandad punched Mother Free-Spirit in the mouth twelve years later. I still remember the pitiful sound she made when Grandad realized she wasn't going to allow him to push her down the stairs. Free-Spirit was having a manic episode and venting an ancient grudge she carried since childhood. Her father demanded silence. The Painter's shame of domestic abuse had manifested prior to this when Regular told me Free-Spirit once hit him in the face and begged him to hit her back. Catching him off guard during what was expected to be a romantic evening at the beach, Regular grabbed her hand after the blow. She said his hitting her was the only way she knew he loved her. Naturally confused, he repeated "no" and attempted to reason with her. She said her parents used to fight a lot. After a few minutes, Free-Spirit tried to hit him again, but this time he restrained her before she could make contact. Sound familiar? Mr. Alone told me he became exasperated and took her home immediately, despite Free's pouty objections. The Painter and Alone households had their respective shares of dysfunctions.

Nevertheless, Regular carried me into my grands' bedroom while Sweet and at least two of my uncles, Muscle and Might, were clamoring around me, claiming that my father was keeping me from them. Mother Free-Spirit argued with her younger brothers until Grandma finally told them to stop reaching for me. I clung onto my father for dear life; I somehow knew my anxious uncles wouldn't have held me properly. In hindsight, Mother Free-Spirit and Grandma must have been a

Voice and Valor

little possessive of me as well. They all favored themselves and insisted that Regular turn me over, accusing him of keeping me from them. I remember him becoming defensive as he demonstratively held me away from his body. Clearly, I was clawing his shirt, not wanting to be separated ever again. Despite favoring my grands, I knew this man was my father and that he had my best interest at heart.

Two years later, my hero appeared in my hospital room after I'd broken my leg. Regular was handsome, tall, dark-skinned, and I always remembered his easy smile and deep voice. I didn't know it at the time, but he was unhappy at home growing up and had left to join the United States Army as soon as he was of age. Regular hadn't revealed his intentions to his own mother until two days before his scheduled departure for boot camp. Still, nobody made me feel like my dad did. To me, he could do no wrong.

I may have been enraptured by the television or asleep when I suddenly heard "Hey, son."

Voice and Valor

"Daddy!" I exclaimed. Regular swaggered into the room, walking past the small window overlooking the nurse's station. Leaning in, he smiled real big too, and gave me a hug and a kiss on the cheek. I was ecstatic but confined to the bed with my right leg bent and suspended from a harness that was attached to the ceiling. He held a small teddy bear out toward me.

"I got you this."

"Thank you." I was overjoyed but didn't know how he knew I was in the hospital. My greatest hope was that he didn't know *why* I was there. Toxic shame — I was prepared to be sad and ready to turn on myself.

"Your Aunt Gabrielle told me you had broken your leg and was in the hospital. So, I had to come see you." We laughed as he said, "You need to stop jumping off them porches. But I know you won't." He seemed proud of me at that moment.

While in my thirties, over a card game of

Voice and Valor

Crazy 8's, we bonded and counted our similarities. Regular told me he had broken his leg around the same age, playing Cowboys on a chair. This man also tried the flute but was primarily a percussionist. He told me Free-Spirit told him I chose the flute on my own, and I revealed her lie. I used to long for my parents to be together, but their reunion always ended with her fussing at him while he stood in silence, ready to leave. My own bond with Mother Free-Spirit was awkward growing up. Connecting with Regular soon became difficult as well. Nevertheless, I would have been great at sports, especially basketball, because he was a neighborhood sensation. My uncles tried to teach me, but they turned me off due to their unfair expectations on my "natural" talents. They applied pressure on me to be like my father, the living legend of the projects. Muscle's and Jew's coaching styles were over-zealous, self-centered, and inept.

Regular stayed and talked to me a good while before deciding he had to go. I stole a peak at my grands as they checked in at the nurse's station. He must have caught a glimpse of them as well, but he didn't appear hurried.

Kissing me affectionately on the forehead, Regular said, "Bye, Son. I'll see you again soon."

"Nooo, I don't want you to go," I moaned but understood. Our bonding was to be postponed once again.

"I'll be back again to see you." We smiled at each other, and he walked out.

I heard some muffled, angry chatter outside my door then a sudden silence. Regular's footsteps resumed and became faint as Grandma emerged with a forced smile, Grandad with a determined look.

Over another distant future game of Crazy 8's, I told Regular what I remembered about the encounter I slightly overheard at the children's hospital. I had wondered why my hero never fought for me to be with him over the years. He told me

Voice and Valor

Grandad had warned him to never come see me
again… at gunpoint.

Voice and Valor

"Shame has been called the master emotion because as it is internalized all the other emotions are bound by shame. Emotionally shame-bound parents cannot allow their children to have emotions because the child's emotions trigger the parents' emotions" (John Bradshaw)

Voice and Valor

"Dante, come here! I think I see your dad!"

That cloudy Saturday morning, still half asleep, I sprang from the pallets to join Cousin Quincy, 13, at the living room window. I, age 14, assumed he had heard the neighbor's door shut and two people walking down the steps.

Furrowing a skeptical brow, I pushed aside the other sheer curtain next to Quincy. We looked down at the street. There he was! Butterflies turned in my stomach as I observed the most intriguing man I knew in motion. He was talking with a strange female who was laughing as they climbed in what I ascertained to be his car. They pulled away.

Quincy and I looked each other in the eyes in near disbelief. He knew, more than everyone else, how I continually asked Regular's mother and siblings if they'd heard from my father. They usually told the truth; "No." Quincy and I were beyond excited, but it was more surreal to me. We must have been making enough noise to attract our

Voice and Valor

hosting Cousin Darlene's attention. Quincy was lucid enough to give me a supportive glance before dashing off to our host's side to let her know what we'd just seen. I texted Quincy while writing this to ask him what made him look out the window initially. He said that he recognized my father's car. Regular and his brother, Quincy Sr., were close.

Our instincts told us he and his lady friend were coming back some time that day as we knew this wasn't where he lived. He was in the army, so Regular Lee Alone had to have been visiting. But, why hadn't he told me he was in town?

Needless to say, my cousins and I resolved not to leave Darlene's apartment all day. We took turns glancing out the window for his vehicle and/or pausing to hear activity at the neighbor's door. I was going to fight to see him, if it came to that! Finally, early that evening the moment of truth arrived.

I don't remember all the details, but I recall

Voice and Valor

his shock and smile, all of us hugging him, the pleasantness of Darlene's neighbor, and the short conversation and laughter we shared. Soon, Quincy looked knowingly at me, and he diplomatically suggested I have some private time with Regular. Butterflies again. His girlfriend asked to take the car, so she was already gone.

We sat alone together under the opening in the wall separating her kitchen and living room. A yellow-orange glow illuminated our surroundings to spite the overcast skylight.

He didn't know how he could have told me that Grandad told him not to ever come see me. Instead, Regular's withholding this information made me think he didn't care about me.

No one is able to awe and jar me in the same breath like Regular. Still, hoping for the best, I asked, "So, if you hadn't seen me here at Cousin Darlene's, would you have come to my grandparents' house to see me?

Voice and Valor

"No."

His flat, cold, singular response literally dizzied me. I remember nearly blacking out, holding my head down in shame, and the blow to my adoring, 14-year-old heart. I wiped away a tear while writing this part.

I was incredibly desperate yet simultaneously mindful not to disrespect my elder, but I had to know.

"Why not?" Slowly, I looked up at him. Regular wasn't looking at me but absently staring toward the door. I still had his attention. He appeared half here and... somewhere else. In hindsight, I detected pain and anger in my dad's voice and body language that had nothing to do with me. But at that age, any kid would be confused and enraged, wanting to know what he'd done so wrong to deserve abandonment, not to mention such bluntness.

It was a fuzzy encounter, and I know his

reply registered intense avoidance and contempt. The thing about my dad's personality is that he instantly makes you feel comfortable; his masculine charm generates admiration. But, true to his brand of introversion, his lists of reservations amplify his strongly principled self-centeredness. I knew not to press him.

The shaming history surrounding my existence generated profound rage in him while his disconcertedness made me take his negative reactions personally. I remember feeling powerless and strongly desiring to satisfy the longing in my soul. Why was he treating me this way? What wasn't he telling me?

Less than a month before I wrote this section, he told me had a mild stroke. This, of course, frightened me more so than him. His phone was acting up and not allowing his calls to come through during his brief stay at the hospital. Now 40, I was well able to contemplate the severity and ramifications of all this and suggested we have the mature, uncomfortable conversation, tighten up loose ends, and be done with everything should tragedy strike. Thankfully, Regular is recovering nicely, but our conversation about rectifying the misnomer infuriated him.

I'd also asked him about the insurance policies, curious about how I'd be contacted. I was genuinely wondering if I would have to take care of his final expenses should the need arise. He felt like I was trying to kill him off, despite my saying we need to have this hard talk before it's too late. Regular hated it, growing steadily angry as we shifted to a more tender topic.

"I'm not worried about getting no name changed on a birth certificate after 30-something years!"

"40!" I corrected. He paused, I believe, in embarrassment and refusal to submit to my request.

"I still don't see the need to do all that. You know I'm your father."

Voice and Valor

"Yeah, but why wouldn't you want to square things away with your son before anything worse happens? My grandparents are gone, mom wouldn't be an issue, and this would be between you and me, father and son. Every past obstacle is no longer an issue!"

It would be decades before I learned about Grandad and the gun at the hospital, about the fake name for my father they created on my birth certificate, and the emotional games played to deter Regular from staying in contact with me. When I was small, Grandma detained me in her room while Regular and Grandad fussed at each other downstairs. She was restless. I knew what was going on; they arranged for Regular to come over under the pretense of signing the necessary paperwork to change the father's name on the vital statistic.

Grandma retrieved the articles from a large wooden chest saying, "We've been trying to get him to sign these for years."

Voice and Valor

At my young age, I was fully aware she was telling me a half-truth. He was right downstairs. I remember repressing signs that I wanted to see him for fear of disappointing my grands. Intelligent, I also knew their fear that I'd choose to leave if Regular had pressed for custody.

Furthermore, Mother Free-Spirit (a number of years later) detained me in a closed room while Grandad argued with someone standing at the living room door. Once the yelling concluded, Mother released me after checking to see if the coast was clear. I raced to the den, eagerly awaiting my dad's arrival to pick me up to take me to his wedding. Grandad had been the enforcer in response to my mother's jealousy of Regular's decision to marry Holiday.

Mother Free-Spirit stood periodically in my peripheral. From the hallway, ten or more feet away she said, "I guess he's not coming."

I had been alternating glances between the

analog bicentennial clock and the rainy window for what seemed to be an eternity. My caregivers knew what they had done but were too ashamed to confess their antics.

Honestly, I don't recall when I realized he was the one Grandad met at the door. Regular much later confirmed he and Uncle Quincy Sr. had in fact come to get me that dreary day. My father, indeed, bears a considerable amount of pain. This man, like so many of us, are prime candidates for inner healing, and since I have experienced the benefits of it, I desire this for him. Furthermore, according to Regular, and I believe him, Holiday got pregnant before separating to keep him from divorcing her.

"Do you know how I would feel at your funeral, all of our relatives standing there knowing I'm your eldest but the soldier walks up to give Kayla the folded flag? They don't even know I exist. Do you know what you would be putting me through?"

Voice and Valor

Regular paused again. "That's deep. I never thought about it like that." Retreating inward, he continued, "I haven't decided whether I am going to have a military funeral or not."

To him, that was a suitable answer. True to form, my hero couldn't properly understand my emotions because of his inability to manage his own.

"Don't you think I need to know what to do being your oldest child?" I was assertive and reasonably insistent, although I knew I would be rattling his comfort zone.

It was only because I was his son that he allowed me to get him so upset. He cut it off.

"Well, look, your Aunt Deanna or someone will call the military when I'm gone, okay?! They will be told who to give the flag to. I'm tired of talking about this because the whole thing is bringing up a whole lot of things I left in the past!"

Frustrated and immensely disappointed, I

Voice and Valor

said, "Fine. I'll drop it."

He countered, "Do that!"

"Later."

"Later."

Difficulties with personal valor, unfortunately, continue to render Regular Lee Alone incapable of fully affirming his own son.

In addition to all this, in early June 2018, my father confronted me about a surprise Facebook picture of me and my partner. Would you like to find out how that went, Reader? Be sure to purchase *Valentine and Victory,* part two to this work.

Voice and Valor

"Being a provider appears to be at the core of a man's identity as a male and as a parent of worth: to be a man, he feels, means to be a provider. Even single men feel this way" (Shaunti Feldhahn)

Voice and Valor

The following unedited text exchange was between my Cousin Lady Sharon (Sweet's daughter), and me:

Lady Sharon (LS): *Good day cuz hope all is well with you. Please understand that I no longer desire the financial responsibility for ensuring aunties light bill is paid monthly. I will be transferring the bill into her name & requesting that you ensure her light bill is paid monthly. Please forward me your address as soon as possible so that I can set up the monthly statement to be sent directly to you. I haven't told auntie because I made the decision on today and also i don't want her to worry or stress. I can let her know if you want me to that you will be covering her light bill once I*

233

Voice and Valor

solitify the transfer. In addition
My husband & I are still unsure
of when we're moving. Aunties
lease ends in October & will not
be renewed. Prayerfully by then
we will have found a big enough
space for her to come back &
live with us. I will continue to
check on her, pay her cell
phone, ensure her rent is paid
for monthly & give her pocket
money. I love you much!!!

You may have already caught the similar titles for Sharon and my ex-wife (Lady). In addition, when had she started saying *auntie*? We all grew up saying *aunt* and *uncle*.

> **Me:** *I thought your mom was*
> *paying the utilities.*

Sharon hadn't consulted me before finding a senior living facility for Mother Free Spirit. Although Sweet received love offerings from her small congregation and occasional honorariums for

Voice and Valor

preaching, she had no dependable income. However, she got the bigger bedroom and agreed to pay the light bill while my mother paid the rent with her disability. Reader, you may have already guessed, I was conveniently made unaware of the move-in date and living arrangements.

> **LS:** *Yes between my mother & I we have ensured it's been paid. However now it's time for that financial responsibility to be released.*

> **Me:** *Who says that? That was a responsibility y'all took on w/o conferring with me initially. I will not allow you or your mother to improperly throw off a responsibility you and her committed to onto me.*

> **LS:** *I said it Dante!!! My mother nor am I are not improperly throwing off anything off on you. You can*

235

Voice and Valor

leave my mother out of it!!!

Lady Sharon is her own mother's enabler. Sweet, while in her late fifties, lost the Painter Family House due to foreclosure where a handicapped Mother Free Spirit and our Uncle Muscle still lived. The Painter family unit moved there the summer I was born, and my grandparents passed away in the late 1990s. I had returned home for some time in 2008 and willingly offered to pay my way since I worked daily. Sweet refused my contributions. She thought of the house as part of her birthright but failed to take a job to sustain the family abode. Ultimately, I was surprised when I came home from a day of school teaching to see that the sheriff had evacuated everyone. I remembered receiving a missed call while facilitating my last class of the day; however, this did not explain Sweet's negligence to inform me of the impending doom.

In shock but still in full composure, I called Sweet to ask her what happened. I asked Sweet why

Voice and Valor

she hadn't told me we were in danger of losing the house. Allowing her pride to fuel her negligence, she forwent her responsibility to give me fair warning. I remembered thinking it weird that she had been spending the night elsewhere weeks prior, always taking with her the cherished dresses she got from Katherine's and a few other items. It was as if Sweet was internalizing judgment day and sneakily moving out.

She must have become visibly overwhelmed by my reasonable inquiries, prompting Sharon to grab the phone. The daughter came to her mother's defense. I was freshly irritated by Sweet's uncanny knack for avoiding confrontations, especially when she caused them. She struck me as an extremely emotional immature, middle-aged woman who only acted "like an adult" when involving herself in other people's matters. When accountability knocked on her door, Sweet would often run for the hills or hide behind her evil daughter. Calmly, I warned the almost-five-years-my-junior Cousin Sharon that this

Voice and Valor

was between her mother and me, and that unless she wanted a problem between us, then she should put her mother back on the phone. Lady Sharon's voice elevated and became sterner. I wanted to curse her out but held back knowing my mother's well-being hung in the balance. She yammered something, reminding me she had a right to defend her mother. She hung up in my ear, not before saying, "What's done is done. I got this. Your mother is with me, and they will live with me."

No matter your best intentions, it's difficult to prevent fighting with someone who is immature and spiteful. Cousin Lady Sharon is very jealous, enormously insecure, and overly competitive, always seeking approval even if she has to step on you to pull herself up. I also learned about the "avoid/criticize loop" in one of my organizational leadership classes where people avoid verbalizing their criticisms about you *to* you, but talk *about* you behind your back — maybe even *at* you in person. This is the behavior pattern of too many people

Voice and Valor

when they disagree with something/one. Unfortunately, Lady Sharon was taught how to do this by Sweet. However, Sharon took it a step further and would use any hearsay against you.

Beyond irritated by my loved ones' ignorance, I still tried to be mindful that God was concerned about how I handled myself.

> **Me:** *And, who do you think you are? You told me your mom was paying the utilities, so that's gotta be handled decently and in order. Mind your attitude. You're being bossy, and I will not work with you under those conditions.*

> **LS:** *I'm not going to battle with you Dante!!! The June 22nd bill will be paid and everything from there is on you... Please forward me your address to ensure you receive the billing statement. I will follow up with*

239

you regarding the details of the name transfer.

Me: *This is a battle you shouldn't have presumed. Many of the issues I've had concerning my mother's well-being originated with your mother. You defended her, unnecessarily involving yourself as usual.*

Me: *As I stated, you're being bossy, as in over-bearing. You will not disrespect me.*

LS: *At the end of the day Dante your mother is your responsibility!!! You have been quite blessed to have the support regarding her. As I stated keep My mother out of this!! Please forward address....*

Me: *Your mother is in this despite your constant meddling.*

Voice and Valor

*Have a great day. Don't text me
again with your foolishness.*

LS: *Whatever Dante just be
responsible & take care of your
mother's light bill. This is not
about me or my mother despite
your foolishness of speaking all
this craziness to me.*

Me: *You can be blocked...*

LS: *The choice is yours!!!*

Me: *[smiling wink face]*

While trying to figure out how to block her,
Sharon's texts kept coming through. Her contempt
reminded me of the last time I had stopped over to
see Free Spirit. I didn't visit often due to financial
struggles and not feeling comfortable around my
mentally-ill mother, the nasty Lady Sharon, and
phony Sweet. Free was occupying Lady Sharon's
dining room area with her queen-sized bed, armoire,
and other possessions. My credit was under repair,
and I had neither yet obtained year-round income

241

nor my own place. It was weird that Sharon, her husband, Second Husband, their five children, and Sweet were not home on an early Saturday morning.

I opened the unlocked front door a crack and said, "Ma?"

"Yes? Dante? Come in."

Mother Free-Spirit couldn't move around a lot due to her physical condition but sat waiting for me in her bedroom. I could hear her radio as I drew nearer to the curtain separating the living and dining areas. There was a strange aura about the house, striking me as if an argument had just ended. Apparently, Holy Spirit was letting me know what had happened a half hour or so before I arrived. When I inquired of Mother Free Spirit where everyone was, she told me Second Husband had to forcibly get Lady Sharon out because my cousin didn't want me over "her house."

LS: *You should be ashamed of*

Voice and Valor

*yourself!!! I pray the Lord deals
with your heart & convicts you
severely.*

Me: *He's judging you too. God
shows no favoritism.*

LS: *Your absolutely right and I
know he's judging every pure
intention & sacrifice that I have
made and he will bless me, more
than abundantly.*

The block activated successfully. I
proceeded to Facebook and prevented collaboration
there as well.

Lady Sharon and I grew up in the same
house as children, and although I was her older
cousin, for all intents and purposes I was practically
her elder brother, Smooth her younger. As children,
their parents (Sweet and Spicy) believed Cousin
Smooth and I picked on her because she was the
only girl. Smooth and I were too young to combat
their reasoning but much later agreed that our

elders' assessment was incorrect. Authentically, Smooth and I resented young Lady Sharon because she was "grown" (always rolling her eyes, back-talking, and using a disrespectful tone of voice when addressing others), received far less spankings than deserved, and manipulated her mother out of the few restrictions she was put on. We boys were forced to endure long tenures in our rooms for misbehavior. Smooth and I didn't always get along because I was the typical, bullying big brother to both of them; however, we were on the same page when it came to Sharon.

We often ~~teased~~ *taunted*, her about her weight, knowing it would get to her. They finally started pointing out the size of my nose. You can only imagine the hurt feelings and the subsequent bickering akin to our sibling life. Still, we're adults now, all three well past 30 years of age. One would think that we'd be able to treat each other with mutual respect and, at least, communicate fairly to resolve old/new problems.

Voice and Valor

Sharon became — rather presumed herself — my mother's caregiver. I practiced vulnerability and confessed my deepest embarrassment that I could not provide for Mother Free-Spirit. I wished I could have had an amicable conversation with Sharon; nevertheless, her haughty, nasty attitude prevented that.

In truth, I rarely used the *b-word* to refer to a woman…until it suddenly became necessary…

Voice and Valor

"A big part of the [communication] problem… is that women do not realize how different men are from their female friends." (Belinda Elliott)

Voice and Valor

I once lived in an apartment with Mother
Free Spirit that was still in Sharon's name, and my
handicapped maternal figure lived there alone.
Again, the previous arrangement was for Sweet to
stay with her and manage the utility bills while
Free's disability income took care of the rent. It
wasn't long before Sweet moved out and was
staying with her daughter, Sharon. So, needing a
residence, I moved in and began taking care of the
power and gas bills and shared my food stamps with
my mother. One day, the gas stove had
malfunctioned; the pilot light was still on.

We texted.

> **Me:** *Hey, cuz. Please call the
> maintenance crew because the
> stove has stopped working.*

> **LS:** *Are you working it
> properly?*

Reader, did you raise an eyebrow? I too felt
her question was insulting. Growing up, I used to

cook for and with her and used to live in an apartment in the same complex months before this. *How dare she?*

> **Me:** *Of course, I know how to work the stove. Why would you ask me something so insulting?*

> **LS:** *I was asking you what maintenance would have asked.*

> **Me:** *You can't presume what they would ask...*

I was getting irritated, but managed to hold my temper.

> **Me:** *...Just please stop by after you leave work so you can see what I'm talking about.*

I don't remember her responding. A couple days prior, Mother Free-Spirit and I got into an argument, and she'd called me a son of a bitch. Insulted, I looked at her and said, "Well, if I'm the son, then who's the bitch?" You know, Reader, that if she could spit fire on me, I would be writing this from a hospital burn unit! LOL! However, she glared at me and continued loudly fussing even after I was no longer in the room. Around this time, Free had once again come off her psych meds and was manic. I remember one instance where she loud-talked herself into hoarseness but kept yelling at me because she "wasn't going to let the devil shut up one of *God's prophets*." My bedroom was upstairs, and I could hear her voice echoing through the under-furnished apartment, despite the closed door.

By the time Lady Sharon arrived, "the prophet" had been silent. Sharon inspected the stove. She was visibly annoyed when she realized my conclusion was correct. As I attempted to express my concerns about her condescending text, Sharon became dismissive, rolled her eyes upward, and tended to her phone as if I was getting on her nerves.

I paused.

Voice and Valor

"Why are you acting like that when I'm trying to talk to you? Do you see you're being disrespectful?"

"Dante, I don't have time for this. I just got off work." She continued to sigh, roll her eyes, hum, and play on her phone.

"Bitch, who do you think you are?!"

That got her attention.

"What? What you call me?"

"You're acting like a bitch, all rude when someone's talking to you. You don't roll your eyes and pay attention to your phone as if people ain't worth your time."

Mother Free-Spirit came alive.

"You see how he talks to women? He makes me sick!"

My use of the word "bitch" in a separate conversation with Free had no real bearing on my encounter with Sharon. Although I felt the sting of my mother's betrayal, I ignored her and the fact that she'd numerously bad-mouthed her niece, the very one she was defending against her own son. Reader, we've often heard that blood is thicker than water, but estrogen seems to be thicker than blood, if you'll tolerate the analogy. I learned this first when Sweet and other females turned on me upon hearing the lies Lady O told about me.

Cousin Sharon walked past me, placing her phone to her ear. She was calling her mother and husband to come over from a city away and resumed talking down to me when she hung up.

"It's amazing how people who ain't got a pot to piss in or window to throw it out of…" — this is a phrase Lady Sharon copped from Grandma when our deceased matriarch grew weary of her grown children still living there, not contributing financially, and eating up everything — "…feel like they can talk to you any kind of way! I need to go ahead and put your ass out."

Voice and Valor

I countered, "Oh, and that's fine because I expected you to say that next. You think you can act like a bitch and not be called one?"

This phenomenon reminds me of the observations of *Comedy Central's* Trevor Noah on how many American people dislike being called racist but do/ascribe to racist things.

Mother Free Spirit burst into sobs. "Oh no, Sharon, please don't put my son out! Pleeease!"

Game over all of a sudden? I rolled my eyes internally at Mother Betrayer, ignored her pathetic pleas, and firmly communicated my stance to Cousin Lady-Bitch.

"Just because I'm living in your house doesn't mean you can treat me any way you want and think I'm not supposed to feel some type of way. You need to go home and talk to your husband like that because I ain't him!"

I had let her know.

Voice and Valor

Instinctively, I knew that Sharon disrespected her husband. Second Husband's temperament is weaker than hers, and he too was "walking in his deliverance." My own suspicions about Lady Sharon's own bisexuality and extra-marital affairs, ironically, were confirmed to me in September of 2017 after I'd finished contemplating reasons why we couldn't get along. Again, people who fixate on certain "sin issues" tend to project them onto others. Apparently, she and Second Husband had strong feelings for the same woman who informed me.

Despite Second Husband's awkward physicality and super-spirituality, the king didn't deserve the verbal abuse he endured from the queen of his castle. Second Husband and I were similar in that we found it difficult to be the man of our own houses when living with a self-centered, over-opinionated woman. Females like Lady Sharon pick fights out of fear of being dominated and end up treating their men like doormats. Like clockwork,

253

Voice and Valor

Dr. Emerson Eggerich's *crazy cycle* begins.
Eggerich aptly stated that when women don't
respond respectfully, men respond unlovingly.
Then, when he attempts to put his foot down, the
disrespected husband comes off as cold. As Belinda
Elliott noted, "Men and women are simply wired
differently,".

Yet, too many women would fail to admit
that they use their marriage/relationship to stage
feminist protests and pick fights with innocent men.
Good men are lumped in with his chauvinistic
counterparts and accused of not being
understanding.

The biblical King Solomon knew what he
was talking about! Straight men understand the
impossibility of living blissfully with contentious
women. It turns out that even men trying to live
straight find this very difficult as well — nothing to
do with sexual preference after all, huh, Reader?
Again, some women are simply "bad guys."

Voice and Valor

Unfortunately, I couldn't talk to Second Husband candidly though; I'm not attracted to him but always wanted to warn him about what he was getting himself into with my cousin. Second Husband's own arrogance and his having been brainwashed by Sweet and Sharon pushed me away. I also believe that the shame of allowing Sweet to manipulate him away from a genuine female love interest and into an arranged marriage to Sharon weighed on him continually. People often become addicted to not only chemical substances and sex, but also approval. Religious individuals desire nothing more than to please God, except leaders like Sweet believe that pleasing God is equivalent to doing what she said.

Maintaining wisdom, however, dictated I trust Holy Spirit with Second Husband's journey so that he too could grow his own brain and balls. Religion and/or stigmatization complicate self-actualization. This is why people live lies. Shame, the toxic version, causes us to divide our own selves, according to the late educator and counselor John Bradshaw. Thus hypocrisy, ignorance, denial, fear, cliques, and polluted consciences add to personal and collective confusions about God, ethics, and self-identity. My sincerest prayer for Second Husband is that he acknowledges the compromises he has had to make to forsake his authenticity.

Everyone needs inner healing. Soul wounds jeopardize our sense of fulfillment as well as our relationship with ourselves, others, and God.

Back to the main story… Lady Sharon paced the apartment as if reclaiming her territory. I went upstairs to pack my things. Were Sharon and Free expecting me to hunker down and allow myself to be mistreated?

"No, Auntie, I'm not going to be disrespected in my own house. Uh-uh, Imma bout to show him who the bitch is."

I heard her from below. "Yep, that's you!"

Voice and Valor

I called the woman I was dating at the time to pick me up, so I could spend the night at her house. She was living with her parents who were gracious enough to lend me their couch.

By the time my ride arrived, I came downstairs and saw that Sweet and her son-in-law had arrived. I quickly pleaded with Sweet to not allow Sharon to put my things out. Lady Sharon was upset that she hadn't said anything to me about how I'd called her a bitch. They were standing outside. Sharon called the police.

While visiting Mother Free-Spirit in May 2017 at a mental hospital, she confirmed my notion that Lady Sharon often berated her husband in front of their kids, emasculating him when she lost her temper. Free had lived with them and witnessed many of Sharon's explosions where she threw out the house furniture, leaving her family of eight to have to sit at a long kitchen table in their den. My cousin had been beyond dramatic and unreasonable since childhood.

Voice and Valor

Still Sharon, because her occupation involved social services, possessed connections to assist my mother, and I later expressed my appreciation for her doing so. I efficiently avoided discussing the under-handed, mean-spirited manner in which she assumed my mother's care. Practicing wisdom and humility doesn't always feel comfortable, but the 40th division of Psalms taught me that no one gets away with anything!

Unfortunately, the volatile cousin used my inability to provide shelter for my mother against me, "angelifying" herself and demonizing me to other family members. Can you imagine the pregnant pause over the phone when I told her I knew (from experience) she was back-biting me? Aware of my struggles with financial credit, Sharon criticized me. We later got into a heated discussion about her decision to open a secret bank account with my mother when Free Spirit received a land settlement check. Sharon presumed I would use Mother Free's disability funds and settlement to pay off my debts. As it turns out, Sharon ended up being later reprimanded by a social worker for declaring all of Free's money as income for her and Second Husband's household.

Moreover, God had to heal my heart toward personalities like Sharon's as He created all types of extroverts and introverts. Choleric temperaments, according to a number of studies, are the least appreciated of all due to their destructive, cruel, and people-using tendencies, although their useful strengths include being commanding, strong-willed, determined, and oriented to tasks. I took on Sweet's horribly judgmental attitude toward people with this temperament even to the point where Holy Spirit had to teach me that none of us are *weird*; we're all just *wired*. This is a key principle in DISC studies. Hippocrates' humors described sanguines as bright, cheerful, friendly individuals who are often weak-willed, undependable, and flighty if unhealed. The latter personality is closer to my own.

Ironically, Sweet's doctorate is in Christian

psychology. However, Reader, I'll have you to know that she vehemently believes Lady Sharon is a sanguine, and I am a choleric. Sweet's strong delusions and incessant denials seem to make her resist the reality that she birthed an individual who bears the temperament she despises. Lady Sharon is, nevertheless, the monster her mother created. Simultaneously, Sweet dislikes me to a considerable degree due to her delusion that I am strong-willed. As you read before, Sweet believes she "knows" me.

By the way, I tested Sweet months before editing this section in June 2018. I mentioned to her that I was writing an autobiography. Sharon and Second Husband have seven children (four by him) and are currently separated. Reader, why did I learn from Cousin Lydia that the hyper-competitive Lady Sharon, on Facebook, posted that she was writing a book about her life?

Yes Reader, my eyebrow is raised, and my eyes are on you. We get it.

Voice and Valor

There is a positive form of competition, and this is not it! One-upmanship was taught to us as children, following some of us into adulthood.

Voice and Valor

"Man: Its oldest meaning is 'of the human race.'"
(Manhood Maleness Masculinity — What is
Maleness?-- Graham Reid Phoenix)

Voice and Valor

His eyes were downward as he said, "I don't know what Dante is going to do when he has children. He won't have anything to teach them."

All of a sudden, a normal conversation among college brothers became about *sex* and *gayness.* We had a male singing group called Valor and sang well together until the fear of singing falsetto triggered an intense homophobic discussion that weighed on the rehearsal. I was the only one of the four who didn't regularly meet to play basketball.

Instantly, I stood aback, feeling that familiar abandonment and betrayal I'd experienced all my life. Redd and the guys suspected I was non-heterosexual back at the university, although I couldn't have accepted it until this time in my life. He made me feel rejected the most. Reader, have you ever felt as though *you* were the elephant in the room? We all knew what he was hinting. Why is it that too many people, upon suspecting that a person is gay, find it difficult to continue treating gay people the same way they would any other human being? With men, it's too true that if you can't talk to the next guy about sex and/or sports, then conversing about anything else feels "weird."

I discerned Redd had had this discussion with the other guys when I wasn't around. I am quite certain it was he who secretly elected himself to be the jerk who was going to "expose" me. Ironically, he was/is one of the most narcissistic of us all, often openly admiring his own form, especially his "pretty" feet and hands.

Annoyed at society's narrow-mindedness of manhood, I was resilient when I responded.

"There's got to be a whole lot more to manhood than playing sports, man. I'm willing to be taught if you're up to teaching me. We're brothers in Christ and doing that shouldn't be a problem."

My logic took some wind out of his sails. I was aware that spending too much quality time with me even to teach me basketball would endanger his reputation. Homophobia dominated his psyche.

Fear is irrational and self-centered. *What does this say about me or what will people think of me if I show I am okay with him/her being gay?* Soul search: Don't those questions sound crazy? Your conscience is asking: *What do you look like acting out against someone who isn't mistreating you?*

Shame can cause others to project onto others how they feel about themselves. Jesus, for that matter, didn't care about what the religious teachers thought of His being around outcasts (see Luke 15:2). No, I'm not taking this scripture out of context. Many Christians would love to accuse me of this, but we recognize that religious and traditional people tend to resist truth and cling to comfort zones. Senselessness is senselessness, despite who's preaching it. If Jesus didn't do it, then we shouldn't either. Maybe we need to take another, deeper look at *WWJD* (What Would *Jesus* Do?).

Voice and Valor

For the aim of *Voice and Valor: An Autobiography for Re-humanzation* someone else's being hetero- or non-heterosexual has absolutely nothing to do with the next person. We've been trained to mistreat LGBTQIA people differently, trying to protect our own image at any cost, regardless of how we make the other person feel. Christian love teaches us to *show* love to everyone. Love isn't prideful, unkind, or easily provoked. There are no accounts of Jesus casting out a gay demon.

Again, homosexuals are too often considered weak and are deemed worthy targets for harassment and belittlement. However, this is a grave stereotype—risky business! As a thinking human being, I must ask: Where are the *strong* or -regenerated non-gays who are secure in themselves enough to speak up in homophobic conversations? And, we consider gays *weak*? Something more to think about:

Romans 15:1-6a of The Message (MSG)

Voice and Valor

reads as follows:

> *Those of us who [consider*
> *themselves] strong and able in*
> *the faith need to step in and lend*
> *a hand to those who falter, and*
> *not just do what is most*
> *convenient for us. Strength is*
> *for service, not status. Each one*
> *of us needs to look after the*
> *good of the people around us,*
> *asking ourselves, 'How can I*
> *help?' That's exactly what Jesus*
> *did. He didn't make it easy for*
> *himself by avoiding people's*
> *troubles, but waded right in and*
> *helped out. 'I took on the*
> *troubles of the troubled,' is the*
> *way Scripture puts it.*

Reader, don't get me wrong. Though I'm not an enthusiast, I still appreciate sports. It's just the mere fact that being into them is a top validator of masculinity, and this consummate dis/qualifier causes me bewilderment. Had I applied myself, I would have been a superb athlete, I admit. While athleticism provides a sexy swagger and, in some cases, public fame, sustainable damages to the body and/or brain are a reality. Also, playing sports would have never changed my sexual orientation, which is but a small part of my total identity.

Sometime in 2017, I read a Facebook post where Redd, now a married man and father, asked if people would continue supporting a gospel artist who turned out to be gay. This had occurred within only two days of *Facebook-friending* one another. His own aunt commented cautioning him to leave situations like that between the person and God; he *liked* the comment, but having experienced his brand of hetero-superiority/homophobia, he is unlikely to change. Hmmm… It's common for homophobes to hide their own same-sex attractions with put-downs. I ended up un-friending him, tired of such ignorance. I was on my way to bigger and better things! Had a book to finish.

Voice and Valor

"It happens to everyone as they grow up. You find out who you are and what you want, and then you realize that people you've known forever don't see things the way you do. So you keep the wonderful memories, but find yourself moving on." (Nicholas Sparks)

Voice and Valor

God always looked out for me and counteracted negativity. Even while writing this, He reminds me that later in life He spoke through a prophet saying that I would teach many people many different things. Such words would affirm anyone who knows the agony of bearing an untold story; thank you, Dr. Maya Angelou.

Extending my thoughts on male socialization, women can be inhumane toward each other. Although they characteristically discuss menstruation, menopause, their insecurities, etc. relatively comfortably, men often maneuver life without the freedom to express the full range of their human experience. Most guys don't know a man can have more than one wet dream in his lifetime or that men can often experience andropause (decreased sex drive, diminished testosterone, and over-production of estrogen in their middle years often due to age and/or improper diet). If "*knocking down* as many women as you can" is the hallmark of manhood, then can you

imagine the shame of admitting you don't desire sex
as much as you once did in younger years? My
heart breaks at the silent cries of a man who fears
opening up to male peers. He bears an ignorance to
male physiology, but a strong devotion to sexuality
keeps that old man from teaching younger men
what to expect in life.

I have come to know that prayer (faith
without a corresponding action), push-ups
(exercise), and pussy (sex) cannot solve everything
in a man's life. An authentic relationship with God
is mankind's only solution to fulfillment.

Frowning, Sabrina said, "I am meeting more
and more of y'all who're not into watching sports."
While we were dating, she also once treated me
with contempt upon discovering I grew up without
my biological dad. I've found that this undue shame
is often displaced onto many fatherless men similar
to me as if it was my fault for being fatherless.
Sabrina herself was raised by a single mom.
Society, however, places the stigma of

fatherlessness solely on men. I hope that when she and other women read this, they will take the time to study the available resources on the effects of fatherlessness on daughters.

Surviving social challenges such as those above wasn't always easy. Every man has done things in order to make it through, but I've found that "surviving" is a by-product of an impoverished mind. We were meant to thrive. Thankfully, I have a resting place, and am constantly tapping into the unsearchable richness found in my Heavenly Father.

Each quarter, I request prophetic words from a particular voice — a neutral minister whom I've never met. He digitally records tailor-made messages for my life. I decided to transcribe and interweave his affirming utterances throughout this final section of Valor in order to add more depth to my narrative. In the latter part of 2016, the messenger opened by saying that while praying for and preparing to minister to me, he saw strings

Voice and Valor

attached to my body. He said he did not know what
that meant until God began to speak to him.

Son, in this hour, I am
detaching the strings on you.
It's not [that] you are a puppet,
but the enemy has longed and
desired to control you. He has
longed and desired to make you
a man of the world (independent
from God) to where you begin
to think like the world [and]
function like the world. We're
not talking about drinking,
smoking, and sleeping around
[but] it's the idea of thinking,
the very thought pattern and
processes of the world to know
how to carry out the command
of what a man should be, of
what a man should look like,
what a man should talk like, and
[how] a man should carry out
the commands...

273

Voice and Valor

The *commands.* He repeated that word. I,
like most men, have lived life following orders —
well, duties and common rigid expectations — that
have, honestly, evolved into stereotypes. American
women tend to have a broader existence by
comparison. Having grown up without the
affirmation of manhood by most people in my
family, I developed an air of innocence and
eccentricity and struggled with acceptance
intensely. I was/am physically strong, highly
intelligent, incurably clean-cut, unapologetically
friendly, reasonably handsome, very wise, and
musically talented. Still under the mentorship of
Sweet at that time, I was also super-spiritual. Once
you are presumed as "different," "weird," "soft," or
gay, and especially, non-athletic, many guys readily
presume you are inept at *everything* men do. My
traits must have annoyed/shamed others, making
them feel some need to change me. Recurring
experiences like these often made it easy to develop
ungodly beliefs about myself that God eventually
exposed and healed.

Voice and Valor

Reader, you too believe things about yourself that God does not believe about you. Some of you think you are not smart. This is untrue; the Creator has afforded mankind at least nine types of intelligence, that which is natural to you. He has also availed us spiritual gifts, which are evident at birth but should be cultivated for God's use. Everyone has at least one of each. Unfortunately, many believe when they're told they couldn't do "this/that"; leadership charisma isn't always natural, but like spiritual gifts, other gifts can be acquired. Practice asking Holy Spirit to reveal each one of your self-defeating beliefs, to lead you to discover and cultivate your gifts, to help you replace them with His truth, and to heal and free you. He is the Helper, and we will always need His help for everything. Take it from me and countless others who have grown tired of the rat race of life — the Lord is far more gracious than anyone could ever be!

Going back to that past college experience, I

Voice and Valor

was still trying to find my identity. A thousand thoughts swirled around in my head, but none of them felt powerful enough to combat my friend's passive-aggression at that moment. It reminded me of cruel family members who taught me that my feelings meant nothing. I was often bullied and heckled, no matter what I chose to say. Whenever frustrated by strict notions that I shouldn't talk back to elders, fight family, should stand up for myself, and the fear I looked like a girl while swinging punches, my eyes would water. They took this as a weakness, not knowing my inner conflict.

At age 2, I remember at least two of my uncles—between 10 and 15 years older than me-- mumbling they believed I was going to be gay. Being an overcomer provided me a long memory. I lacked the voice of my earthly father, the one whose guidance should ring in my ears during times of adversity. This prolonged void created a desperation within the depths of my being that only God could fill. My maternal grandfather raised me, but he was

Voice and Valor

old school, felt providing was everything, wasn't developmentally supportive, and non-athletic, but had calloused, ready hands that ruled the Painters with an iron fist. He believed love was demonstrated through work ethic. Neither he nor his sons were mechanical, thus I inherited the same characteristic. I learned how to change a tire and the fluids in my car from someone in school but had no one to teach me how to bob and weave, to keep my head up. You know, "manly" things.

An increasingly transparent Kirk Franklin wrote as the soulful Fred Hammond sang,

> *There's a hole in my soul that*
> *won't heal,*
>
> *and there's a rage and a pain*
> *even now I still feel.*
>
> *And even though I'm a man still*
> *I don't understand.*
>
> *But that's what happens when*
> *you don't have a father.*

Voice and Valor

No one knows the magnitude of the songwriter's words unless they have lived them. While I was raised by Grandad, I was forced to grow up without the influence of Regular, my biological father.

As a little boy, I don't remember many compliments from my significant others. Uncle Muscle laughed at Uncle Jew, who sent me conflicting messages at times. Jew sat down in the living room chair and stood me in front of him. He told me to ball up my fists. I did. In my subconscious, I heard someone say to me, *You look like a girl. You can't fight.* I felt like I was wearing a sign, even into adulthood. Jew balled his huge hands, put up his guard, and told me to swing at him. After doing so, my then favorite uncle devastated me with a barrage of fake punches. He looked at Muscle and joked, "He didn't know where they were all coming from!" I stepped aside, as Jew and Muscle rose and walked laughingly away. Freshly shamed for not having learned how to fight

278

Voice and Valor

at that young age, I stood there angry at myself.

Now possessing an appropriate vocabulary, how was I to learn from someone who was supposed to be teaching me valor without humiliating me at the same time? Jew's version of toughening me up was antagonistic, opportunistic, and sarcastic, not to mention extremely intimidating. I was a child. He was a teenager that was bordering 18 years, my uncle, and a Painter elder. Yet, if I spoke up for myself or had struck him, I would have been yelled at and punched onto the floor. I understood the necessity for learning self-defense, but my uncle's tutelage on everything as usual, including sports, didn't register as authentic. Most importantly, I learned much later in life not to think like "them" about myself. Thankfully, I have long since begun working on my self-talk and made the choice to move on..

Voice and Valor

"Learning involves change. It is concerned with the acquisition of habits, knowledge, and attitudes. It enables the individual to make both personal and social adjustments... (Matthew Knowles)

Voice and Valor

...Son, you [knew] what it was like to be a man of God. You wanted My will and nothing more. Son, there were many times in your life [where] you found yourself in a place where you didn't know what to do; you didn't have anything. You didn't know what you had to do when you had to make decisions. [Even when] those decisions turned out to be bad and wrong, you always came back to Me. You always lifted up your head because you knew 'your redemption draweth nigh.' You knew that in the spirit realm there was something more. You knew you had to think on a higher level. You knew you needed to think like your Father in Heaven..."

Nothing can replace the human factor. A revolving question in my mind was why couldn't so-called "manly" men have real conversations. I recall a present prophetic female friend telling me that people would rather gossip or talk at you than have a conversation because conversations identify them, allowing them to see what's in their own hearts. I'd ask myself, *Would they feel like they were wearing a sign?* Promoting healthy communication brings maturity and growth. No

281

Voice and Valor

wonder we have people in their seventies who are immature and others like them who are set in their ways. Listening and hearing out stigmatized individuals nullifies the hoopla, but homo-fear, for example, keeps people from realizing they're majoring in the minors and minoring in the majors. Jesus Christ was saying this when He told His audience that He was from Heaven while we were from Earth.

The Son of God lived, died, and rose again so that we could re-humanize.

As I think back on my encounters with the suspecting few, I realized I was a scapegoat for a number of them who were secretly struggling with their own identity. After my divorce from Lady O, I, against my better judgment, allowed unstable Uncle Pierre to live with me. I didn't know it, but Pierre had crept down the stairs and saw me hugging a male friend in my dark living room amid the blue glow of my TV screen; we had just finished praying. This friend later came by and prepared a meal for me when I fell ill. Pierre witnessed everything but the prayer and asked me if was I gay. I, in turn, asked why he'd ask such a thing. In the same conversation, I decided to practice coming out. So, I told him I was "struggling" with it. He, while drunk, stereotypically assumed my sexuality was why I divorced Lady O. Because Pierre bore the label of being the Painter Family Black sheep, I imagined ignorance, misery, and shame drove him to reveal my secret to a number of our relatives while in his thousandth drunken stupor. Of course, venting disgust at my "lifestyle" (a demeaning buzz word) secured his own reputation. Little did he know that his ex-girlfriend told me she witnessed him once living in a rooming house amid queer men.

A daunting truth is that manhood is in a crisis. If you ask 100 men what it means to be a man, you'll get 100+ different answers. Women think they know too, never mind the fact that they have never lived one day as a man, yet want to weigh in whenever any male of any age fails to meet her expectations. Meanwhile, I remember drowning under the waves of contradicting voices, desperately needing guidance from my eternal God because so far these fellow humans presumed much more than they could truly offer.

At the age of 35, I had a telephone life-coaching session with the same prophet whose words are interwoven in this vignette. My weariness at self-hate prompted me to confess my pangs at being validated spiritually while feeling divided about my unshakable sexuality. He told me he wasn't like most life-coaches and that I must be confident in who I am. This wise, prophetic voice taught me that sexual attraction is a law just like any other, and no one can help to whom they are drawn. I learned that I can control my conduct but not my orientation and attraction. His words set me on a liberating, sometimes scary journey, toward self-love and rediscovering God's unconditional love for me. Fighting to attain self-confidence became my pursuit.

I am most grateful for the higher-level counsel I received from this incredibly accurate prophet and successful entrepreneur. Having "studied to show [himself] approved," he was the one who introduced me to *What Does the Bible Really Say About Homosexuality?*. In it, I learned that because heterosexuals can't get beyond their "icky" feeling, they equate that *feeling* to mean homosexuality is wrong. The opinion that it is "gross' means something's immoral. Doesn't it make sense that a person who doesn't like liver cannot understand why another person craves it? Acceptance is key.

Sexual *orientation and attraction* is natural and in accordance with one's wiring. Sexual *conduct* is the only aspect we can control.

Moreover, Dr. Helminiak educated me on the biases of Judeo-Christian thought. Its fixation on male same-sex activities was not a moral issue,

285

believe it or not, but simply because Israel was trying to increase her population in addition to preventing sexual practices for idols. To Judeo-Christians, same-sexual behavior between females was actively ignored. In their minds, it was not considered sex because there was no genital penetration. Women were thought of as barely more than "orifice bearers." Perhaps, this is why many men defend their hetero-bias, unwittingly offending women, and regard females solely as procreative/sexual objects.

In the 15th-century, Henry Cantor recklessly exploited Levitical passages referencing male homosexuality, and his observations led to the 16th-century persecutions of homosexuals (similar to the divisive hysteria of witch hunts). Same-sex practices were considered normal, according to the history of sexuality. Sex has no history, but sexuality does. Among many other things I had to unlearn, Helminiak's book decoded words such as *ceremonial/ritualistic*, *abomination*, and *un/natural*,

Voice and Valor

revealing most of all that the word *homosexual* wasn't introduced into the Bible until early in the 20th century. Again, Levitical passages were not meant for everyone. If that were the case, then men could never shave their heads or beards. A menstruating woman could not be in the same house with her husband until her flow was dried. While these and countless other ordinances are routinely reconsidered as "traditional," too many Christians hold onto the *homosexuality* passages with a self-righteous vengeance. I, myself, once did until I began to think independently. Anyone paying attention would realize there's something wrong with how LGBT people are treated.

With regards to "un/natural," what feels natural to one person may not seem natural to another. Take two little girls and stand them at a table with a doll and a basketball. What if both females walked away with a toy, respectively. Does this mean the girl with the doll will find happiness in heterosexual relationships? Does this mean the girl who wants to join the WNBA want to have sex with women? Biology/chromosomes and DNA dictate behavior, sexual orientation. Sexual *attraction* is uncontrollable and innate. Sexual *conduct* involves choice. While I am not big on using animals to establish human morality, I have seen YouTube videos about beasts of the field and even water fouls that have formed homosexual-pair bonds. Reader, educate yourself. Find out what God already knew.

When we read Paul's reference in Romans chapter 1, it seems to be a no-brainer if we stop at face value; however, deeper study reveals that the apostle's words referred exclusively to temple prostitutes. As it turned out, men and women at that time were having sex with male and female temple leaders in efforts to ensure a plentiful harvest that year. This behavior was consistent with paganism, a practice God strongly forbade. Historically, being gay and living as a gay person had nothing to do with one's spirituality.

Voice and Valor

I Timothy 1:10 includes *practicing homosexuality* as being contrary to sound doctrine, or God's order. This is another of at least six biblical passages used to condemn homosexuals. Reader, your eyebrows should raise after learning that *arsenokoitai* was used in ancient times, originally translated to mean *a man in many beds, shrine prostitutes,* and *economic exploitation* — inconsistent any way you look at it. The Greek noun was never used to refer to our modern meaning of homosexuality. What if the Heavenly Father already knew what you've just read? One of the writers of *Positively Gay* asserted that bias against gays is worse than the perceived sin. The sad thing is that too many religious-minded people, including non-church goers, would resist this knowledge and fall back into bad habits, therefore doing nothing to change. Traditions die hard, but they must die.

Several emotions churned within me as a growing hunger for truth swelled when I discovered that homosexuality in biblical time was a completely different subject altogether for us today. I could finally stop hating myself. Reader, knowledge that the Bible does NOT condemn homosexuality has been suppressed over a protracted period of time for political gain. The definition of *politics* is the "activities associated with the governance of a country or other area, especially the debate or conflict among individuals or parties having or hoping to achieve power." Many heterosexuals have a "team" mentality. Gays are then arbitrarily perceived as a societal threat when our counterparts are truly antisocial and non-spiritual.

Furthermore, accepting these truths is not a betrayal of the "religion." God never changes, and He already knew that same sex attraction, as discussed in the sacred canon, are entirely different from our thoughts today. I too had to accept this as truth and unlearn the traditions in my heart. God wants us to study, to be diligent, and to make it our personal business to please Him, not others, so that

290

we can responsibly communicate God's thinking. The biblical passages referring to "gay" activities read as a no-brainer. However, once we've done our due diligence, our ignorance is revealed. The wrong people have been demonized and ostracized for all the wrong reasons.

The golden rule of history is to never place our modern-day mindset in ancient texts because words change their meanings over time. For example, while substitute teaching a social studies class, I facilitated a short lesson on archaeology. The study identified what cavemen called a blade (a sharp, wooden device used for cutting); contemporary individuals would define a blade as a sharp, metal device. However, unlearned people could potentially read the word "blade" in a prehistoric context and instinctively misinterpret. Immature contemporaries have even twisted the same word, creating "gay blade," another gay slur.

Biblical ideologies on same-sex relations are distinct from what we talk about today, while there

291

Voice and Valor

is no getting around Levitical mentions of mixed linens, slavery, or "withered hand" (referring to handicapped individuals). Yes, a person with Bell's palsy and/or a crippling condition would be considered abominations to God. I once read where these same people would have been deemed witches in ancient times. It was considered socially unacceptable to be left- handed, believe it or not. Reader, can you better see why we MUST continue to learn, relearn, and unlearn?

Why do we mistreat people who haven't done anything wrong to us? *Learned behavior*: We upset ourselves about what we assume, imagine, or think someone else does in their private time.

Reader, please re-read the previous paragraph again even slower. Isn't homophobia senseless? Aren't racism, sexism, and all other social prejudices just as stupid?

A YouTube pastor, Dewey Smith, fearlessly condemned the hypocrisies of Christians who throw

Voice and Valor

Holy Bible at homosexuals. He asserted that God wants us to realize we're beating up gays because of the words found in Leviticus right after we've just had some catfish and lobster. According to the same book, consuming shellfish is also an abomination. He also daringly confirmed that the story of Sodom and Gomorrah wasn't about homosexuality either. Again and again, I hear that the issue with Lot's fellow citizens was about a lack of hospitality, not gayness. The Son of God referenced this too when He mentored the disciples on how to handle rejection when going door-to-door to share the gospel. Dewey and our Christ agree that we should never *antagonize and evangelize at the same time!* Such higher-level ideas synergized my realization that neither Jesus Christ nor the Ten Commandments offered an opinion on homosexuality. Therefore, there was no law against being gay. Paying special attention to Jesus's perspectives, Matthew and John were disciples who wrote their gospels many years apart from each other. Mark's account is widely accepted among theologians as Peter's gospel. And, Luke, a physician-turned-historian, walked around gathering stories about Jesus hundreds of years after Christ's death. Any wonder there were no reports of Jesus advocating the screening out of gays, even among His twelve male disciples? Moses, who captured numerous Levitical abominations, never ranked homosexuality among adultery or any other hyper-sexual act on the sacred stones.

Notwithstanding sexual responsibility and self-control, demonizing non-heterosexuals is indicative of hetero-supremacy and is an extension of White hegemony. Some non-gays are diametrically opposed to the existence of homosexuals. Some insist on *Adam and Eve* and not *Adam and Steve* or *Eve and Evette*. Some heterosexuals are "okay" with gays being who they are, but remain uncomfortable with the idea of gays having sex. It is a logical fallacy to assume all LGBT people are sexually active and enjoy all the same pleasures. Conversely, all heterosexuals don't engage in oral sex, and far less straight women enjoy anal intercourse. I was floored when I realized Paul in I Thessalonians 4:11, NIV instructed us to *mind your own business.* His admonition registers to today. When we define people's character by their sexual preference, we violate ethics, distort relevance, de-humanize, and confuse spiritual matters.

This contemplation cultivated an even deeper relationship with Holy Spirit and fostered self-love and an insatiable hunger for scholarship on the subject. I also discovered the documentary, *For the Bible Tells Me So,* which provides intimate details about how people and families reconciled their faith and sexuality in conservative America. A devout Christian mother's eyes were opened to her hate-speech and regretted how she had pushed her lesbian daughter away after learning her offspring had committed suicide. *FTBTMS* continued expanding on the "icky" feeling people experience. A preacher-mom said she realized that when she discontinued imagining how her gay daughter was having sex, she was able to maintain closeness with her adult-child.

The preacher-husband, however, candidly spoke to an interviewer saying he had two prayers for his children as they were coming up; "Lord, don't let my son become no faggot, and don't let my daughter become a whore. He answered my prayers, but He reversed it!"

I imagine the interviewer smiled as the preacher-dad wheezed with laughter.

The *DL's Chronicles* humanized the fear of the down-low (DL) man, featuring fictional stories about Black males who secretly slept with men and validating their reluctance to reveal their truths, respectively. By the way, why is the *DL* label restricted only to African American men and not extended to Whites and females who are secretive about their same-sex attractions? *DL* isn't deception for the sake of deception, according to the apt executive producers. Who would come out of the closet knowing his audience would be hostile? Again, what rational human being would choose a life that would potentially disappoint loved ones and simultaneously change his/her entire world? No one wakes up one day and *decides* they're going to be gay.

I once heard someone say that behind every stigma, there is always something deeper. If homosexuality is a spirit, then we must ask ourselves why are there so many with it today and in history? Let's try not to split hairs. Integrally speaking, I openly confess Jesus Christ is Lord and have never had a possessive encounter with a supposed "gay demon." I've been attracted to both sexes for as long as I can remember, having never asked God for my sexuality, spiritual gifts, intellect, or any other attribute.

When conversing with gay Christians, I often share my discoveries with them in efforts to help them reconcile with God, if need be. Many felt pressured to forsake ~~God~~ the church in order to be true to themselves. Dogmatic Christian leaders have run too many people from the church and caused others to "hate" God and Holy Bible. The truth is social outcasts mistakenly, yet understandably, equate God's attitude with that of His representatives and conclude that their Creator despises them. Indeed, I used to quote "love the sinner and hate the sin" with a sense of superiority before I grew up. Saying it allowed me to feign godly affection while never being honest with the true condition of my heart. Like too many hetero-bias Christians, I used to cloak my arrogance and alienate people who didn't "sin" like me. Of course, this was before I came to terms with my own sexuality. The Bible tells its followers to be impartial and to love without hypocrisy.

Sweet once presumed to give me advice, but I knew someone had to have schooled her about her self-righteous attitude. She displaced, "You can't pray for *and* judge someone." Let's really talk about

Voice and Valor

"having it both ways."

God's love is authenticated in our manners. In the wake of Bishop Eddie Long's death, I had never witnessed so many mean, judgmental Christians. I used to be like a lot of them and decided to ignore the glaring fact that my profession that God loves everyone was the exact opposite. The enemy had, in fact, tricked me into believing that expressing disdain was necessary and if I didn't, that automatically signified I "approved" of the "sin." Homophobia, indeed, involves an irrational fear of what it says about oneself when confronted with gay issues.

Contrary to pompous Believers, people aren't stupid and know when they're getting lip service. We should never practice insulting each other's intelligence. The Godkind of love — *agape* —, unconditional love, is not based on performance. Christians who elevate homosexuality as the "big sin" are fooling themselves, irrational in their thinking, and are often compensating for some inner void.

"The church is the worst place to go if you have a problem. They are supposed to be showing love. I don't wanna serve their God," say countless outcasts. We've forgotten God and have turned "different" people into problems. The same God who gave us His Son and our spiritual gifts also gave us a brain and free-will. Applying knowledge is godly. Misapplying it is not.

Whether or not we understand these studies, it is important to realize that God watches how we treat people. No one can run from their conscience.

Voice and Valor

*"How beautiful maleness is, if it finds its right expression... (*D. H. Lawrence*) [Manhood Maleness Masculinity — What is Maleness?-- Graham Reid Phoenix]*

Voice and Valor

...[Well] done, thy good and faithful servant! You have decreased, son. You've allowed me to increase in your life. You've allowed that same Spirit to dwell in you, to quicken you, and begin to speak to you. Son, I want you to know something today [and that is] you've become the Superman of the hour. How do men become the Superman of the hour? They begin to understand how to decrease. They begin to understand 'not my will, God, but your will be done.' They understand the process of what [the] true manhood anointing should be like. And the mantle of a man [is] and what that feels like. Son, you've done that. You've become a friend of God like Abraham did. You've become a man after Mine own heart like David did. You've studied to show yourself approved. You knew in your heart there is something more to this life than what you're doing, just working and just doing this and doing that. Son, your decisions were never based on the ideologies of man(kind)..."

A word I'm coining is *re-humanize*. We are very familiar with dehumanization, inhumane, humanitarians, human rights, and other "human" terminology. However, men, in particular, need to

302

Voice and Valor

be allowed to slow down and connect themselves with their own humanity — human *beings*, not human *doings*. I learned this when studying biblical meditation, "be still and know" that God is God. Our hearts are blind. We can and need to be delivered from ourselves. The book of Genesis also tells us that Elohim made mankind to be a "living soul," a *speaking spirit*. I believe American culture, in general, has repressed human males emotionally and spiritually, transforming "manhood" into a myth, creating enormous inconveniences for countless people. Maleness is first and forever humane.

Superman, how ironic — considering my childhood fixations on Wonder Woman. LOL! I fully accepted the reference and relished in the character's original emulation of Christ. Think about it; a powerful baby alien raised by earthly parents. They knew who he was long before he did. Selah. As an aside, I'm writing this vignette in mid-May 2017. Would any of my readers be surprised if

Voice and Valor

I told them one of my Painter uncles called me with a corny crack about the June release of the movie about the most famous amazon? Well-meaning, I guess, but really? I turn forty-one in the fall.

One of the voices in *For the Bible Tells Me So* said, *There's nothing wrong with having a fifth-grade understanding of the bible as long as you're in the fifth grade.* I no longer say that I believe every word that is recorded in Holy Bible.

I was determined to win my battle against traditional and religious thinking. A proper, objective education on the issue of same-ex attraction was extremely important to me. One of Wayne State University's professors said during his talk entitled *What's Morally Wrong with Homosexuality* (on YouTube) that God is never wrong, but some men have gotten Him wrong. The Ph.D. aptly stated that male biases crept into certain passages. Like him, I don't ascribe to throwing the Bible out or picking parts I like and throwing out parts I despise. However, fairness and "rightly

Voice and Valor

dividing the word of truth" is always in season.

My unique vantage point and destiny forced me to take an honest look at the "infallible word of God," as we Christians assert. While I don't ascribe to the ancient Catholics' monopoly of the Bible, I see why they would have believed the scriptures shouldn't be interpreted by the common man. The sacred canon is for conscious, critical thinkers. Slavery passages, second class treatment of women, and more, reveal traits which are similar to White hegemony (WH). Here again, WH is a westernized ideology that says that if you are not a Caucasian, wealthy, heterosexual, Christian male, then you are defective. Anyone who fails to meet one or more of those standards experiences disenfranchisement more or less in the United States of America and in other parts of the globe. WH's very premise is made-up. It's highly limiting, illusory, and dehumanizing, to say the least. Just as no one chooses to be born on Earth, no one *chooses* to be White, Black, Asian, Indian, or any other race.

Voice and Valor

However, we can *choose* ignorance. Therefore, no one has the right to claim supremacy over anyone!

The audacity of White supremacy, long before slavery, asserted itself as legislators of God's will, if not as God-figures themselves. Anthony Stanford's *Homophobia in the Black Church: How Faith, Politics, and Fear Divide the Black Community* connects Black cultural resistance toward homosexuality and follows the trail of faith-based funding to the pulpit of Black mega-churches. It also spotlights how members of the Black clergy have sacrificed Black LGBTQ Christians for personal and political advancement. The author pulled back the curtain on Black alliances with White social conservatives as well as religious and political extremists in his 2013 book. Dissecting and dismantling the construct of WH is everyone's responsibility.

I stated in a previous section of *Voice and Valor* that I once read that one of the top fears among men is that he is gay. Men, in particular, are

Voice and Valor

notorious hypocrites, especially with regards to their own emotions due to the effects of de-humanization. For example, I'm reminded of a game show where a contestant/professional athlete had to confess in front of his wife and the world that he peaked at another man's penis in the gym. He was, of course, caught off guard by the question, but the premise of the game was to tell increasingly harder truths for money. We all would know if he had attempted to deceive because he was connected to a lie detector. He was noticeably uncomfortable as his reputation and respect from his beautiful wife was on the line. If he answered no to protect his ego, then we would have all wondered what he had to hide. If the masculine, attractive husband told the truth, would his wife still think less of him? He was integral, admitted he looked at the guy's genitalia, and advanced toward higher lucrativeness. His wife had a short moment then nodded, blinked away childish assumptions, clapped, and rooted her man on. My point? It's human to look. The problem is, homophobia turns normal looks into a lustful stare similarly to how "thoughts" are confused with desire. I can only imagine the backlash he received in the days ahead, however.

Homo-fear nags the human soul. Being called a girl always works in curbing a male's behaviors and vulnerabilities. Why is that? "You throw like a girl" stings the male ego a little more when a girl outruns an over confident boy, or when an unknowing, straight man learns he was defeated in an arm wrestling match against a gay man.

Moreover, Dr. Rudy Payne's *Understanding the Framework of Poverty* taught me that poverty is not ethnic, and that in a culture of poverty, as opposed to middle class opportunities or affluence, the stereotypical mindset is that a "real man" is a lover and a fighter. Since I was not thought of as a fighter, many "sneaky" Christians suggested I get more "pussy" to man me up. This added even more contradictions to my then 20-something-year-old mind. Imagine my surprise 10+ years later when I found out that Jesus Christ affirmed the existence of

Voice and Valor

eunuchs, some born or made that way and others who chose to live that way; we would consider them contemporary asexual individuals.

Biblical teachings forbid fornication, but even saved boys and men were "winked at" when they violated this principle. Even though I never slept around, I and the girls I was exclusive with were very sexually involved and faithful. Carnal/worldly pressures to prove my manhood and to "be a man" often ran deeper than ordinances on purity. Even though no one was going to just "beat my ass," guys seeing me with my girlfriend helped me escape most physical altercations.

I came to know that hyper-masculinity wears down the precious human soul.

Bearing all this and more in mind, I inadvertently decreased as the prophetic word declared because I, more than ever, realized my and the human race's desperate need for Holy Spirit of Jesus Christ. We need Him living inside us to produce genuine love, joy, peace, patience, kindness, goodness, faithfulness, and self-control. One can only bow his/her knee and confess His Lordship after allowing Him to personally reveal to us His peaceful intentions for humanity. Furthermore, stepping away from religiosity, not Jesus, enabled me to observe the Son of David authentically. He set me on a new course, one that will inevitably rattle the cages of African-American homophobia, homophobia in general, and Christian two-thousand-year-old traditionalism. I discovered in my doctoral studies that Jesus was logical, a novel idea to those of us determined to attack intellectualism.

Moreover, Jesus said that when we witness His actions, then we are observing His Father in action. There are several reasons why the God of the Old Testament seems different from the One we see in the New Testament, but I will only mention a few. Prejudices caused the over-emphasis on homosexual activity in Sodom and Gomorrah. They were destroyed because of a lack of hospitality. Don't believe me? Compare Jesus's mention of the cities and the context in which He speaks about them when sending His disciples out door-to-door and two-by-two. Also, the book of Ezekiel mentions the numerous sins of Sodom without highlighting same-sexuality. Popular preaching over-emphasizes and brainwashes, subsequently making it difficult not to read into passages (insert subjective, popular interpretations). Many theologians agree that homosexuality as addressed in the Bible is different from what we are talking about in the contemporary world.

History also reveals how the mean and cruel inhabitants left strangers out in the cold, excluding them from human decency and warmth. Bearing this violation of hospitality in mind, Helminiak described the true sodomites as those who are cruel and inhumane, past and present. Sodomy took on a new meaning, as colloquialisms and slang often do. Today, it's commonly used to refer to those who are

Voice and Valor

believed to engage in oral and anal sex — a true perversion (*twisting*) of the original meaning. It is true that the hatred and biases against non-heterosexuality is worse than the evils associated with consensual homosexuality.

Sexual battery, moreover, was but one way the inhabitants of Sodom and Gomorrah humiliated their visitors. I cannot resist recalling "buck breaking," where White American slave masters often raped male, African captives in order to subjugate them and invited their White traveling guests to do the same. We're familiar with notions that slave women were sodomized, but many of us are unaware that even Black men were raped by White masters. What better way to subjugate a person's soul? Rape doesn't seem to always be about sexuality, but power and control.

Dear Reader, there is truly nothing new under the sun, even regarding sexually violating either sex. The book of Judges tells a story involving gang rape, dismemberment, and body part messages. Only this time it was a girl, who was left at her father's doorstep. Closer studies at stigmas and human atrocities usually uncover the toxic shame of the oppressors. A truth — bullies being tormented by their own demons while unsuccessfully finding inner peace — they inflict their soul hurts onto others. Some turn on themselves and develop strong addictions. The problem is, pride won't allow them to be honest with their own secret pain. No one escapes their conscience. I have found that love, not just hatred or indifference, is the polar opposite of fear. Indeed, the oppressed and their oppressors need inner healing for themselves and their ancestors.

Jesus Christ, love incarnate, came on the scene, liberated all social outcasts, and turned several Judeo-Christian Levitical laws ("the bible" in its day) on their heads. His intentions were to reexamine the laws, without destroying them altogether, and to reaffirm the eternal truths stated by His prophets. Moreover, the "big sins" we fixate on today are inconsistent with the overall spirit of the sacred canon. Jesus Himself was quoted saying that blasphemy against Holy Spirit is the single worst and only unforgivable sin — not even suicide counts under this declaration. Who but God can determine someone's eternal destination? Many non-heterosexuals have killed themselves after enduring prolonged rejection from family members, cruel peers, prejudiced strangers, etc. because fearful, hate-filled humans made life here unbearable for them. God, in His infinite grace, is smarter than all of us. Just ask the Pharisees… and the modern-day ones too. Again, I believe Holy Bible is a book which must be handled by critical thinkers, not pious, over-zealous copycats. While I will never "throw the baby out with the bathwater," I am careful not to take the best-selling book at face value.

Voice and Valor

"The illiterate of the 21st-century will not be those who cannot read or write but those who are unable to learn, unlearn, and relearn" (Alvin Toffler)

Voice and Valor

Many of us are brainwashed and unaware of it. Hosea and Elihu (in Job) declared that humans die without knowledge. On the other hand, Paul said knowledge without genuine love puffs us up. Balance and priority are everything.

Close-minded Christians think and believe God feels threatened when we use the brain He gave us. I discovered this when pondering Jesus's assertion that we render his word powerless when we hold onto traditional thinking. Holy Spirit is also a teacher; with His light, He challenges us to critically examine even our strongest beliefs. For instance, when we take to heart what the preacher says without ever studying the scriptures on our own, we usually end up developing a tradition/religious argument that conflicts with God's input.

Moreover, the Lord is continually re-teaching me what it means to be a "living soul." Our soul supplies us with, among other things, an identity, feelings and an intellect; however, when

Voice and Valor

we disregard self-love and unconditional love, we damage not only our own souls but also that of others. Society taught us to respond viscerally, meaning to react emotionally and without thinking. I studied Jesus and realized He wouldn't have shunned me and that taboo is merely symptomatic of inhumanity... and traditionalism.

I encourage my readers to glimpse Tim LaHaye's books on males and their personalities so that they can find out why we all act the way we do. His wife, Beverly, also wrote a version for women. Via Reverend Tim LaHaye's examinations, particularly, we can see that God made men of varying temperaments, biblical ones included, in His own image. We are of various psycho-emotional extremes, ranging from very sensitive to emotionally under-developed. America tends to celebrate/validate one type over others, which was never God's intention. Nevertheless, each temperament affirms all types as male-men. When I contemplate how angry women rarely hesitate to

Voice and Valor

tell a male he's not a man when he fails to meet her expectations, I can't help but flip the logic to make a point. To us, women don't stop being "women," even when they behave overly aggressively toward us. Why is male identity so easily attackable? We need transformation, to re-humanize on all sides.

The decisions you made [and had to make in your situations] were never based on things that were worldly. Ever since you accepted Me as Lord and Savior, your decisions [have] always been based on 'Lord, whatever you want. If it's to take away from me; if it's to add to me; if you want me to act like this, if you want me to do this.' All you wanted was My will and My will only. You've become the hero, ...the man in My

Voice and Valor

book, the Lamb's Book of
Life. You will begin to speak
on a different wavelength. All
that matters is that you
detach [this world's
systematic] strings that have
been placed on you...

Stigmatized individuals are often treated as
if they do not count. This attitude is
counterproductive to the heart of God for even Jesus
that the last shall be first, and the first shall be last.
When I initially heard that Jesus never spoke out
against homosexuality, in particular, I was still in a
frozen mental state. The prevailing, hardening
notion — rather, traditionalism — taught me to
immediately combat Christ's omission with
spiritualized bigotry. Yes, Jesus is The Word, but
even Paul's words sometimes conflicted as he
matured in his walk. Looking at that truth
objectively began to thaw my mind. My personal
truths squared themselves hotly against me, forcing

me to deepen and look this man in the mirror.
Intelligent observation of the world around us and
the scores of disenfranchised individuals like me
caused me to step back and begin utilizing the mind
He gave me. I tapped into the frequency of my inner
voice, and finally began hearing the voices of the
most courageous people I have ever known. A
friend taught me a saying in September 2017:
"Never pick on the gay ones because they've been
fighting all their lives."

In fact, it wasn't until I stopped going to
church for a while that I truly began hearing the
voice of the Spirit of God. Ironic, isn't it? You'd
think that I would be able to hear Him easier in "His
house" considering all my years of listening to
preachers, prophecies, gospel songs, etc., and even
my own preaching. When I visited again, to support
a pastor friend, I was freshly reminded as to why I
had discontinued going to religious services. An
accompanying minister female friend was forced to
agree. Religiosity is a huge turn-off to anyone

Voice and Valor

who's tasted genuine freedom.

My soul longed to be free, although being alone and/or wondering if there was anyone else willing to be honest often perplexed me. I knew God hand-picked me since before birth. He created me to be cerebral. The Lord chose my gifts, talents, and trials and tribulations — all of which were to shape me for His purpose. Yet, having been inundated with religious rhetoric and the tyranny of expectation, perception, and self- rejection, I struggled toward a comfortable level of self-acceptance and self-actualization in my walk with Christ and my identity. Studying to show myself approved, as Holy Bible prescribes, set me on a path that not too many people have found... or, at least dare to "come out" and admit.

While privately tutoring a woman in English, we read Frederick Douglass' autobiographical *Narrative,* where he said:

In moments of agony, I

Voice and Valor

envied my fellow-slaves for their stupidity. I have often wished myself a beast. I preferred the condition of the meanest reptile to my own. Any thing, no matter what, to get rid of thinking! It was this everlasting thinking of my condition that tormented me. There was no getting rid of it. It was pressed upon me by every object within sight or hearing, animate or inanimate. The silver trump of freedom had roused my soul to eternal wakefulness. Freedom now appeared, to disappear no more forever. It was heard in every sound, and seen in every thing. It was ever present to torment me with a sense of my

Voice and Valor

wretched condition. I saw
nothing without seeing it, I
heard nothing without
hearing it, and felt nothing
without feeling it. It looked
from every star, it smiled in
every calm, breathed in every
wind, and moved in every
storm.

Consciousness — inescapable, nothing like it.

I came to know that the human experience, spirituality (faith), and science were never meant to conflict. However, too many Christians (especially those of African descent as well as lower income European descendants) attack intellectualism, completely forgetting that even the intercessory prophet Daniel was a man of philosophy, linguistics, and administration. Most of the people mentioned in the canon were very well educated. The same Omniscient God Who endowed you and me with spiritual gifts, personality, and other abilities also requires us to utilize the brain He put in our skulls. God never meant for us to be afraid to think for ourselves. It is a by-product of our freewill.

Rethinking what we've accepted as right and wrong, Godly and un-, is parcel to co-laboring with Christ. When we think about it, Jesus had many conflicts with the Pharisees, Sadducees, Herodians, and scribes with regards to the sentiments of the Law (again, the Bible of their day). When considering passages in context with Christ's mention of "little gods" and "eunuchs," it becomes clear that He couldn't say much more than He did. Even Jesus had to bob and weave when dealing with small-minded individuals. Christ knew how His contemporaries viewed tax collectors and prostitutes, but Jesus reached out and did not exclude them. He was conscious, fully aware of the plights of others, His deity, and His humanity. He too was a thinker, not a copycat or blind, religious

Voice and Valor

zealot. Which are you, Reader? *Because meaning perspectives are structures of largely pre-rational, unarticulated suppositions,* according to John Mezirow, *they often result in distorted views of reality.*

I write this because many people (especially resistant prophetic minds) will seek to view what I am saying about the Bible as a direct attack on God. This is farthest from the truth! Stubbornness is symptomatic of Toffler's 21st century illiteracy; we must be willing to learn, relearn, and unlearn so that we won't be un-studied, be unapproved to God, and ashamed of ourselves. My strong belief is that the sacred canon was meant for thinkers and that God is never wrong, but even biblical authors have been and currently get God wrong!

Be careful, Reader, thinking on this level can bring you to a scary place in your thought-life. Nevertheless, this is precisely why we must learn to discern His voice, despite what the pages say. Too many people are in bondage to bad marriages, to unsupportive leadership (women kept "silent"), and more because they simply weren't taught to hear God for themselves. God is never intimidated by our complexities... or progress. Yet, we are!

Jesus was not a conservative but a liberator. He wasn't political or religious. He wasn't even trying to make a statement when He healed the gay centurion's lover. Non-heterosexuality was a biblical non-issue. I met a radical, married-to-a-woman, African-American male pastor in Norfolk, VA who told listeners to return home and shake up their own preachers with the notion that the soldier wanted his slave healed so that he could be able to make love to the boy again. Turns out, it's expressed unabashedly in the original Greek.

It's essential that my readers know that with regards to Holy Bible, I would NEVER "throw the baby out with the bath water." I must reiterate that fact. However, I will encourage us to eat the fish and to spit out the bones. Think—God is not offended by the brain He gave you.

Voice and Valor

Even though evil men use scripture to justify cruelty, discrimination, murder, and rejection, it undeniably prescribes human beings the healthy manner in which they should treat each other on this planet. In tandem with hundreds of past and present scholars, one historian declared that the sin of Sodom was homosexuality, according to many Christians but not according to Jesus and the Bible. Modern preachers allege that God destroyed that it goes against the testimony of history, the testimony of scripture, and the testimony of Jesus. The sin of Sodom and Gomorrah was un-hospitality, not gayness. Learning this, made me incredibly thankful that I didn't have to choose between my faith and being true to myself. I exist as a man of God who happens to be bisexual because of Him. My passion for God, as you could imagine, swelled because He always, always loved me first.

The Creator requires us to show unconditional respect and unconditional love — an inescapable reality to everyone, including strangers

Voice and Valor

(*neighbors*, as He called them). Taking a look at the parable of the Good Samaritan in the gospel of Luke reveals the beauty (compassion) and ugliness (brutality) of individuals. Indeed, we will all be judged by our consciences and held accountable for our actions. Life is God's priority, especially Jesus's, as the Son told a once ill-tempered John and James. I invite you, Reader, to valiantly fight to elevate and to expand your mind. And then keep learning. God already knows the things we have yet to learn.

This writing is meant to help open closed minds, and it is for those who are truly spiritual. Being spiritual, Jesus-fashioned, is vastly different from being religious. I decided a while ago to be my own man, free from religiosity, but I had to start from within. Indeed, we are tri-part beings: spirit, soul, and body. Our soul represents out individuality, that which separates us from everyone and everything in creation. It is composed of our will, emotions, desires, memories, intellect, and other components that give us awareness. We also need inner healing and eternal truth because life can hurt us and cause us to harm ourselves and others. Earthly/worldly wisdom can be good or bad as it is often tainted guidance, but God is highly communicative and loving. He enjoys filtering perfect knowledge through imperfect vessels. Upon embracing this, I did tell the Lord that I only wanted to be what He desired. My vantage point and wiring synergized my thinking about maleness; consequently, I observed several holes in the socialization of males and the females they've influenced. I ascertained that Christians, like me, need to admit that we are over-influenced by cultural trends. This is why I began studying Jesus Christ for myself. He wasn't a conservative, republican, or a democrat.

Popular opinion is not the same as eternal truth or ethics (right and wrong). Conventions evolve, but God does not. He is fully aware that we're ever-learning what He already knows.

Voice and Valor

I recently reviewed *For the Bible Tells Me So,* and one of the voices said, "It is the hatred of women that is the fuel of this whole thing [called homophobia]. When the coach wants to humiliate his team, he calls them a bunch of girls. Why does that work? Because the worst thing you can do to a man is call him a woman. Men who are not men in whatever way the patriarchy wants us to be threaten masculine power, and it's too much to bear!" Learning, unlearning, and relearning enables us to think on a different wavelength. Surrendering to God is a continual process, not a one-time thing, especially whenever He shows us another area of our soul that is not yet deprogrammed from religiosity, traditions, and double standards.

It would be nice to hear how women, especially same-sex-loving females, view being under-scrutinized by hetero-superior males. Why is it that lesbianism is more tolerable than gay male behavior? Our imbalanced thinking never equates to God's logic.

Voice and Valor

Personal bouts with spiritual abuse, for example, wore on my mind, as they do to many of you. Holy Spirit reminded me of Matthew's gospel's *take my yoke* passage. I'm thankful I researched it further and discovered the Message Bible version of this popular text. I invite you, Reader, to do the same. It reads:

> *Are you tired? Worn out?*
> *Burned out on religion? Come*
> *to me. Get away with me and*
> *you'll recover your life. I'll*
> *show you how to take a real*
> *rest. Walk with me and work*
> *with me — watch how I do it.*
> *Learn the unforced rhythms of*
> *grace. I won't lay anything*
> *heavy or ill-fitting on you. Keep*
> *company with me and you'll*
> *learn to live freely and lightly.*
> *(Matthew 11:28-30).*

Anyone ever listen closely to the verses of Kirk Franklin's *Take Me to the King?* — "all

331

churched-out, harmed and abused, no rules, no more religion, I make my choice to run to the Healer I need..." The aforementioned passage from Matthew is, in my opinion, a strong word for world pain. People don't have a problem with Jesus, but those who represent Him seem to interfere way too often. Proverbs states that those who are wise win souls. There exists a fundamental lack of wisdom with regards to non-heterosexuals, in general.

It should now be obvious that Jesus Christ was not exclusive. Mankind created religions, but His expectations for human life conflict with earthly ideologies. The pressures associated with being a man, in addition, can be burdensome. Under the exaggerated weight of cultural rigidities, even Bishop T. D. Jakes has said that many men have dropped out of the race called manhood. A memorable exhortation at *Manpower* revealed that men need to be allowed to simply "be" and not just "do." He is pressured to be the provider, protector, lover (whenever his wife isn't denying him), head

Voice and Valor

of the house (but often not really), the hero, everybody's furniture mover, mechanic, counselor, attender of their child(ren)'s school events, decoder of his woman's emotions, and his own defender when forced to take full responsibility for the dysfunction of his household. I have discovered that any of these duties alone are fine within themselves, but if he is deficient in any of them, then his "manhood" is scrutinized. Control comes in many forms. I invite my readers to take a step back and re-examine why men are more susceptible to heart attacks and substance abuse.

Real men diligently fight to protect their own souls, and they care about the souls of others. All men need God, unconditional respect, loyal support, and sexual attention. Allow my repetition of scholarly voices such as Shaunti Feldhahn and Dr. Emerson Eggerichs as they assert these as desperate needs which can never be down-played or over-simplified, even singularly. Readers may cringe at some or all of these fundamentals.

Voice and Valor

However, upon accepting his make-up apart from a woman's, we can see why manhood, centrally, requires re-humanization. Critical women must realize that men are men 24/7/365, despite what he does behind closed doors, his fanaticism about sports, or if he grew up macho. Men, as a race, have been socialized in a manner which limits us from expressing the full range of human emotions, bottling them up, until we are allowed to let them out during "manly" events. Let's all stop being afraid of human, God-given affections, and be courageous! Let God be his judge.

Most importantly, regardless of someone else's volition, we, as men, women, boys, and girls, must valiantly give ourselves and each other permission to find our authenticity as each of us re-enter the human race.

Hear again these words from I Corinthians 13, NIV:

If I speak in the tongues of men
or of angels, but do not have

Voice and Valor

*love, I am only a resounding
gong or a clanging cymbal. If I
have the gift of prophecy and
can fathom all mysteries and all
knowledge, and if I have a faith
that can move mountains, but do
not have love, I am nothing. If I
give all I possess to the poor
and give over my body to
hardship that I may boast, but
do not have love, I gain nothing.
Love is patient, love is kind. It
does not envy, it does not boast,
it is not proud. It does not
dishonor others, it is not self-
seeking, it is not easily angered,
it keeps no record of wrongs.
Love does not delight in evil but
rejoices with the truth. It always
protects, always trusts, always
hopes, always perseveres. Love
never fails. But where there are
prophecies, they will cease;
where there are tongues, they*

*will be stilled; where there is
knowledge, it will pass away.
For we know in part and we
prophesy in part, but when
completeness comes, what is in
part disappears. When I was a
child, I talked like a child, I
thought like a child, I reasoned
like a child. When I became a
man, I put the ways of childhood
behind me. For now we see only
a reflection as in a mirror; then
we shall see face to face. Now I
know in part; then I shall know
fully, even as I am fully known.
And now these three remain:
faith, hope and love. But the
greatest of these is love.*

II Timothy 4:7 & 8 (NIV):

*I have fought the good fight, I
have finished the race, I have
kept the faith. Now there is in
store for me the crown of*

Voice and Valor

righteousness, which the Lord,
the righteous Judge, will award
to me on that day — and not
only to me, but also to all who
have longed for His appearing.

Hebrews 12:1 (MSG):

Do you see what this means —
all these pioneers who blazed
the way, all these veterans
cheering us on? It means we'd
better get on with it. Strip down,
start running — and never quit!
No extra spiritual fat, no
parasitic sins. Keep your eyes
on Jesus, who both began and
finished this race we're in.
Study how he did it. Because he
never lost sight of where he was
headed — that exhilarating
finish in and with God — he
could put up with anything
along the way: Cross, shame,
whatever. And now he's there,

Voice and Valor

in the place of honor, right
alongside God. When you find
yourselves flagging in your
faith, go over that story again,
item by item, that long litany of
hostility he plowed through.
That will shoot adrenaline into
your souls!

Re-humanizing one, never forget that you
are human before you are a man, woman, boy, or
girl — human *beings*, not human *doings*. Allow
yourself to be human. Get in touch with your spirit
(identity in Christ), soul (individuality, will,
emotions, intellect, memories, imagination, desires,
etc.), and body (health and wellness). As you
continue to learn to love the person in your mirror,
don't forget to teach others to re-humanize as well.
What we do (to ourselves and others) affects our
souls. No more regrets, only re-humanization.
Beside Holy Spirit, it is the answer to stigma.

I pray that you decide each day to become

Voice and Valor

21st-century literate — always learning, relearning, and unlearning—follower of the authentic Jesus Christ!

(I realize that not all of my readers are Christ-ians; however, the truth remains that if our deity does not prioritize life, then we are serving a monster.)

Luke 9:55-56, NKJV says, "But He turned and rebuked them, and said, 'You do not know what manner of spirit you are of. For the Son of Man did not come to destroy men's lives but to save *them...*'"

Voice and Valor

Epilogue

Voice and valor are inalienable to any human being's rights. In fact, God would be disappointed at us for not fully radiating the light He put within each of us, not to mention His anger at our smothering His light in others. Life is a battle. We should choose to help make everybody's life here easier, and in turn, we can all live without regret. Everyone has something to say and should never merely just want to say something. There's enough ignorance in the world. Let's spread humanity.

Before anyone reaches for their gavel to judge me as a heretic (oppositional to traditional thought), anti-Christ-like, bound for hell, or even demon-possessed, they must ask themselves are they willing to be as brave and transparent as I have? Jesus Christ, to me, is Lord. My strong concern is that His representatives have turned

Voice and Valor

would-be generals in the Body of Christ against God due to our religiosity and unhealthy church culture. The Lord distributes gifts as *He* wills. Again, could prejudice be a large part of why the Body has yet to see revival, miracles, signs, wonders? Anyone paying attention will admit that there gifts present within non-heterosexuals are often not evident in their straight counterparts. We should repent for our blindness.

The real Jesus was in the gospels all this time! And, He is who we all need to follow.

I chose to tell my truth and the truth about The Truth. My stories are a source of strength; ones from which I continually draw nothing but greater self-actualization as I deepen my amazement at the power of God within. The present Dante is much more assertive. No one can hold anything against me any longer! I am free, indeed.

I know who I am, and that reality is empowering, especially knowing that Jesus Christ loves me just the way I am and never would have condemned me. Paul's first letter to the Corinthians, chapter 15 and verse 10 of the Easy-to read Version states, *But, because of God's grace, that is what I am. And his grace that he gave me was not wasted. I worked harder than [most others]. (But I was not really the one working. It was God's grace that was with me.)* It takes valor to be and remain true to yourself as you continue to grow in knowledge and character.

Being non-heterosexual is a gift, not a negative. Let's stop treating LGBTQIAs who love God, in this emphasis, as if they're bastards or step-children. Allow them to sit and eat at the main table with the rest of our Heavenly Father's children. Again, Jesus Christ said, *"I have other sheep that don't belong to this sheep pen. I must lead them too. They will listen to my voice and there will be one flock, with one shepherd. This is why the Father loves me: I give up my life so that I can take it up again" (John 10:16-17, CEB).*

Voice and Valor

Jesus died for the very ones hetero-bias people condemn. Galatians 3:28, AMP, states: *"There is [now no distinction in regard to salvation] neither Jew nor Greek, there is neither slave nor free, there is neither male nor female; for you [who believe] are all one in Christ Jesus [no one can claim a spiritual superiority]."*

Even Paul had to mature in his relationship with the Lord. He once overlooked and seemingly agreed with slavery in the case of the Ephesians but declared there's no such thing as slavery in Christ to the Galatians. Despite Paul's rationale, I respect him as a man of God, a human being who too was trying to grow spiritually and mentally, just like us. Again, no one *chooses* to be straight, gay, or otherwise, and sexuality wasn't thought of in ancient times as we think of it today. However, we all choose our individual behavior.

The ESV of Luke 6:31 makes us rethink, saying, *"And as you wish that others would do to you, do so to them."* Real, re-humanized beings aren't afraid to show empathy. Having read *Voice and Valor*, I hope that my revelations help you to discover your own. The human experience is precious to the Lord. It has a voice. I am sure you found that you could relate to some or all of my stories, no matter your sexuality.

I am an overcomer through Jesus's blood and my testimony! Maybe now you're able to see things a little differently and are able to expand your love walk. Start with family. Look closely at the mirror too. God gave every family the same kinds of people in ample variety (smile). It is my sincere desire that you were stirred in some meaningful way to treat everybody with the dignity and respect they deserve.

Holy Spirit is continually helping me to find/keep my voice and is teaching me true valor. That, to me, is power. I am learning each day to live authentically, holistically, and thoughtfully. Science and faith complement each other, and this truth is exciting. It is my prayer that you will let go of childish thinking and discover the same!

As you continue to learn, relearn, and unlearn, courageously admit that the writers of religious texts missed God on a few topics. This does NOT constitute a betrayal of your faith, however. God is His own person with His own opinion. He is never wrong. People often misrepresent Him. This is one of the main reasons why Jesus came from Heaven to Earth: to show us how His Father thinks.

CAUTION: It may seem counterproductive to allow yourself to feel as if God is falling off His throne when you begin to accept something that conflicts with your strongest belief systems. Rest assured that God can *never* be removed from His supreme station. In truth, what you are sensing is the toppling of strongly internalized traditions…and then, hopefully, if you wait and allow Holy Spirit to speak for Himself, you will sense His warm, welcoming light of truth. God established amazing grace before the world was made. Don't miss your experience(s). You're on your way out of religion/man-made traditions and onto authentic spirituality! Once this begins to happen, you'll re-humanize, and it will get harder and harder to believe lies. Jesus said, "I am the way, the truth, and the life."

Fall in love with the Holy Spirit of God and out of love with religious sermons and harmful opinions spoken on His behalf. Think critically (but don't be petty or obsessive). Your anger should inspire intercession, study, and unifying activism, not self-righteousness and, definitely, not more hateful acts. Invite Jesus to be your chief example, not Paul, your preacher, or the rest. Therefore, if Jesus Christ did not act, speak, or think a certain way, then neither should you. The four gospels are my template for the entire Holy Bible. Never forget that Jesus overturned "The Bible" of His day, and the religious people — Pharisees, Sadducees, and Herodians — those who maintained their traditions, religious views, and self-righteous hang-ups, despite Jesus's teachings.

Choice: Are you willing to become more like Christ or continue to hold onto ideologies that conflict with the Spirit (attitude and 3rd personality) of Elohim? God manifests Himself in ways that we can better understand Him, and He highly values relationships. Will you learn to love unconditionally?

Reader, I am still writing, and I look forward to seeing you again in the pages of my second autobiographical collection to be entitled *Valentine and Victory*. I will get even more transparent as I tastefully expose details of success and challenges with love as well as personal victories over shame. This second part of my life stories will also provide insights about my health and entrepreneurial endeavors.

Voice and Valor

A Lesson in Re-humanization from

Luke 10:25-34, ESV

Voice and Valor

VISUALIZE THIS PASSAGE:

"And behold, a lawyer stood up to put him to the test, saying, 'Teacher, what shall I do to inherit eternal life?' He said to him, 'What is written in the Law? How do you read it?' And he answered, 'You shall love the Lord your God with all your heart and with all your soul and with all your strength and with all your mind, and your neighbor as yourself.' And he said to him, 'You have answered correctly; do this, and you will live.'

But he, desiring to justify himself, said to Jesus, "And who is my neighbor?" Jesus replied, "A man was going down from Jerusalem to Jericho, and he

Voice and Valor

fell among robbers, who
stripped him and beat him and
departed, leaving him half dead.
Now by chance a priest was
going down that road, and when
he saw him he passed by on the
other side. So likewise a Levite,
when he came to the place and
saw him, passed by on the other
side. But a Samaritan, as he
journeyed, came to where he
was, and when he saw him, he
had compassion. He went to him
and bound up his wounds,
pouring on oil and wine. Then
he set him on his own animal
and brought him to an inn and
took care of him."
(biblegateway.com)

Thoughts and Questions

Bringing relevance from *Voice and Valor:*
An Autobiography for Re-humanization, many

Voice and Valor

LGBTQIA people have been abused and murdered. Many (men, women, and children) have even committed suicide due to the shame outsiders put on them. Self-hatred is not inborn.

Bullies often look for perceived "weaknesses" in their targets, thus de-humanizing them. In the parable, what was the sexual orientation of the innocent man? Or, was the man simply a devoted husband of one wife, father, and co-worker on his way home from work on payday?

I looked up "false shame" in Wikipedia. It says this type of shame believes "he brought what we did to him upon himself." Read it again aloud but slower: He brought...what *we* did...to him...upon himself. Absurd, right? Historically, left-handed people were once considered freaks of nature. Should they still be persecuted? Would you as a re-humanizing individual still say "they" had it coming?

People are programmed to hear Sodomites

and think of gay people. However, the robbers in this story are the true Sodomites. These are the types of people who are outright un-hospitable and vicious. Recall: Sodom and Gomorrah were cities full of lascivious, inhumane dwellers. The inhabitants in Sodom intended to gang rape the angels. Consensual sex conflicts with the popular meaning of "sodomy."

Could you, as a re-humanizing individual, turn a blind eye to the actions of the robbers? Some people rob others of not only their personal possessions but also their dignity, promotions, etc.

Now, please don't get it twisted. There are many gay bashers who have had their... rear ends... handed to them. Some non-heterosexuals have had to legitimately defend themselves. Therefore, it's a risky stereotype to assume all LGBTQIA people are weak. We should NEVER under-estimate anyone! I heard about a heckler who was beat down in front of his terrified groupies. Just before they ran away they heard, "Go tell all your friends you got beat down by a faggot!"

As a lifelong learner, I encourage you, Reader, to continually de-program yourself of prejudices and inhumane ideologies. Help those you influence to speak out on behalf of those who cannot stand up for themselves. Become like the Good Samaritan and not like the ones who ignored the ailing stranger. Think like a re-humanized 21st-century literate — learning, relearning, and unlearning.

Homo-sapiens are human beings, regardless of society and hegemony, and come in all shapes, forms, and walks of life. Everyone was at some point someone's bouncing baby boy or girl, then life happened.

For God so loved the world, that he gave his only Son, that whoever believes in him should not perish but have eternal life. (John 3:16, ESV). Targets of abuse always have God and someone else who love them strongly, despite our personal objections to their private lives.

What if everyone made the independent decision to re-humanize — to unconditionally love and respect themselves and each other — as Earth's neighbors and creations of God Himself? Childish (emotionally unhealthy) people don't know that Psalm 24:1 reads, *The earth and everything it contains are the LORD's. The world and all who live in it are his (God's Word Version)*. Everyone on this planet share it together because of God's choices to allow them to breathe on this plane. However, those intent on domination presume who should live or die, be rich or be poor, be free or enslaved. Many powerful people, past and present, are misguided even to the point of assigning one skin color to the slaves and another to slave masters in the biblical canon (Leviticus and Ephesians) and feel America is in danger of God's wrath for deviating from His own plan.

Again, Paul aptly stated, *There is [now no distinction in regard to salvation] neither Jew nor*

Voice and Valor

Greek, there is neither slave nor free, there is neither male nor female; for you [who believe] are all one in Christ Jesus [no one can claim a spiritual superiority] (Galatians 3:28, AMP). Should prejudice have a place in the hearts and minds of re-humanizing individuals?

Finally, consider this passage in Luke 9:51-56, NKJV:

> *Now it came to pass, when the time had come for Him to be received up, that He steadfastly set His face to go to Jerusalem, and sent messengers before His face. And as they went, they entered a village of the Samaritans, to prepare for Him. But they did not receive Him, because His face was set for the journey to Jerusalem. And when His disciples James and John saw this, they said, 'Lord, do You want us to command fire to*

Voice and Valor

come down from heaven and
consume them, just as Elijah
did?' But He turned and
rebuked them, and said, 'You do
not know what manner of spirit
you are of. For the Son of Man
did not come to destroy men's
lives but to save them.' And they
went to another village.

Jesus Christ demonstrated re-humanization to society's outcasts (e.g. the women caught in adultery and the other at the well, lepers, blind-since-birth Bartimaeus, demoniacs, and countless others) when He came to Earth. I am thankful that Jesus came to demonstrate that God's spirit (attitude) toward us is not to kill us. Christ's mindset challenges us to soul search.

Moreover, the Lord's love for us is never based on our performance. He loves us simply because He is love. Finally, while too many of us are excluding (spreading fear, hate, and

Voice and Valor

indifference), God is including (accepting, anointing, uniting, and appointing) people for His purposes. He is longing that we allow His love into our hearts, love justice, and show love and dignity in our everyday lives.

While it is imperative for intelligent decisions on crucial (and some not so crucial) matters, being judgmental is inhumane. Then, all lives will matter just as God intended!

Let God breathe afresh in you and reawaken you to a greater love, anointing, and revelation, free of prejudice. Hypocrisy is a cancer, and it runs deeper than we realize.

Living souls! Re-humanization is everyone's responsibility.

Voice and Valor

Final Thoughts:

I heard the Lord saying, "Yes, I have allowed the reign of this current 2018 presidential administration. And, many of you have seen through the eyes of My Spirit what was to come to past. You have sought me for *what* but failed to seek me for *what's going to happen as a result.* For behold, I have visited America's heart and exposed her underbelly. The Earth needs to see that she is still bleeding, cutting herself deeply to spite her own shame. I have shed My grace on her. Yet, she won't trust Me to forgive and reconcile her. America has deep-seated issues, old secrets which must be revealed. Repentance is vital. I long to heal the ancient wounds, the African-American soul, and the Western mind for I still so love this world. My love equalizes everything and everyone, reminding you all that you are fragile and are in desperate need of the Greater One! So, continue to intercede. Arise with new hope. Renew your minds. And, I will awaken your passion to see Me sweep the Earth with a fresh wind for unity. Receive the attitude of Christ!"

Readers, always remember God is neither a politician nor an Earthling; His Son wasn't partisan. And, He has an opinion outside our own.

Voice and Valor

Sources (appropriate credit given to all quotes throughout *Voice and Valor*)

Berzon, B. & Frank, B. (2001). *Positively gay: New approaches to gay and lesbian life* (3rd ed.). Berkeley, CA: Celestial Arts.

Bradshaw, J. (1988). *Healing the shame that binds you.* Deerfield Beach, FL: Health Communications, Inc.

Coloroso, B. (2008). *The bully, the bullied, and the bystander: From preschool to high school — how parents and teachers can help break the cycle of violence.* New York, NY: HarperCollins Publishing.

Constantine-Simms, D. & Gates, Jr., H. L. (2001). *The greatest taboo: Homosexuality in the black community.* Los Angeles, CA: Alyson Publications.

Douglass, F. (2016). *Narrative on the life of frederick douglass.* Digireads.com Publishing. ISBN 13:978-1-4209-5242-1.

Voice and Valor

Eggerichs, E. (2004). *Love & respect: The love she most deserves; the respect he desperately needs.* Orange, CA: Yates & Yates, LLP, Attorneys and Literary Agents. ISBN-10: 1-59145-187-6.

Elliott, B. *Get your husband to listen to you.* *http://www1.cbn.com/marriage/get-your-husband-to-listen-to-you*

Farber, S., Lencioni, P., & Kelly, M. (2009). *Greater than yourself: The ultimate lesson of true leadership.* New York, NY: Doubleday. ISBN: 978-0385522618

Feldhahn, S. (2014). *For women only: What you need to know about the inner lives of men.* Atlanta, GA: Veritas Enterprises, Inc. ISBN: 978-1-60142-444-0

Freire, P. (1971). *Pedagogy of the oppressed.* New York: Bloomsbury Publishing

Kirk Franklin. (2005). *Hero: Interlude* [CD]. Released October 2005: Kirk Franklin and J. Moss.

Voice and Valor

Kirk Franklin. (June 12, 2012). *Take Me to the King*
[CD]. Tillyman Music Group: Kirk Franklin and
Shaun Martin.

LeNear, Q. & Gossett, D. (Directors). (2007). *DL
Chronicles* [Motion picture on DVD]. United
States of America.

Karslake, D. G. (Director). (2007). *For the Bible Tells
Me So* [Motion picture on DVD]. United States
of America.

Knowles, M. (2012). *The adult learner: The definitive
classic in adult education and human resource
development.* New York, NY: Taylor and
Francis Publishing

Paine, R. (2005). *A framework for understanding
poverty,* 5th edition. Highlands, TX: aha! Process, Inc.

Palmer, P. J. (2009). Circles of Trust: The Work of
Parker J. Palmer [Motion picture on DVD].
(2009)

Stanford, A. *Homophobia in the black church: How
faith, politics, and fear divide the black*

Voice and Valor

community. Santa Barbara, CA: Praeger. ISBN: 970-0-313-39868-1

Trimm, N. C. (2006). *The Rules of Engagement, vol. 2 & 3: Binding the strongman*. Lake Mary, FL: Creation House Publishing. ISBN: 978-1-59185-822-5.

Here's Why Teaching Boys Not to Hit Girls is Only Half Right, Britni, 2014, Parenting.

https://www.youtube.com/watch?v=RLHxNXVXWek. *Black Pastor Does Epic Pro-Gay Sermon.* Accessed October 2016.

https://www.youtube.com/watch?v=5iXA_0MED98. Corvino, J. *What's Morally Wrong With Homosexuality?* Accessed September 2016.

https://www.biblegateway.com/. (All biblical passages in this book were derived from this online source.)

https://www.goodreads.com/quotes/8800-the-illiterate-of-the-21st-century-will-not-be-those

Voice and Valor

http://satpurusha.com/manhood-maleness-masculinity

https://www.goodreads.com/quotes/225913-it-happens-to-everyone-as-they-grow-up-you-find

https://www.youtube.com/watch?v=7OdPr5mvaaY&list=PLYw71iTWovaE5b3_-WUXd7gm_QvfMod2a. *The DL Chronicles, Episodes: Wes, Robert, Boo, and   Mark.* Accessed May 2018.

https://www.wikihow.com/Stand-up-for-Yourself

https://en.wikipedia.org/wiki/Shame

Voice and Valor

Made in the USA
Middletown, DE
01 March 2019